For This Child We Prayed

A compilation of adoption stories

Thomas and Rhoda Bontrager

"He maketh the barren woman to keep house,
and to be a joyful mother of children."
Psalm 113:9

Christian Light Publications, Inc.
Harrisonburg, Virginia 22802

FOR THIS CHILD WE PRAYED

Christian Light Publications, Inc.,
Harrisonburg, Virginia 22802
© 2004 by Christian Light Publications, Inc.
All rights reserved. Published 2004
Printed in the United States of America

2nd printing, 2008

Cover art: Michelle Beidler
Cover design: David Miller
Inside artist: Arlene Shaum

ISBN: 978-0-87813-618-6

Dedicated to all the families

whom God has brought together

through the blessed experience of adoption.

We never need to be without hope . . .

for as we look into the future

with the eyes of faith,

we will see

that God is already there.

—Roy Lessin

Infertility and the pursuit of adoption is a journey—

God walks with us.

Contents

Acknowledgments

We are grateful to:

❖ God. He planned our journey and our family. We have been greatly blessed.

❖ Our children. For their excitement about this project, and being willing to do extra jobs to help it along.

❖ All the families who contributed stories about the children of their hearts. They were willing to share very personal feelings and experiences. Without them there could not have been a book.

❖ All the supportive family members and friends who encouraged our endeavors.

❖ Our church and school family. Their loving support and acceptance has blessed and enriched our lives. They truly believe in serving others.

❖ Arlene Shaum. She changed our mental images into beautiful artwork for the inside of the book. As well as being our friend, she was also a special teacher to a number of children featured in these stories.

❖ Fred Miller. His advice and encouragement was invaluable.

❖ Debbie Forys. She spent many hours typing and organizing this manuscript.

— Thomas and Rhoda Bontrager
63666 C.R. 37
Goshen, Indiana 46528
(574) 642-3600

Preface

This book was not brought into being because we have many answers or because our family is perfect. Rather, because of our many imperfections and the fact that our family is still "under construction," I was very hesitant to pursue this brainchild. The persistent nudging and favorable support of other adoptive parents and my husband did not allow me to put this idea on the back shelf any longer. Fred Miller's encouragement about the need for this type of book enabled me to sense God's continued leading in this endeavor.

Families formed through adoption have a story that needs to be told. Special blessings are often accompanied by special challenges. Such is adoption. The adoption experience is composed of both ecstasy and deep sorrow, struggles, and victories. It is these that can easily be misunderstood by casual observers or even well-meaning family and friends.

Adoption is not a threatening experience. We all may feel rejected and disconnected at times from earthly families. Security and love are not inherited through bloodlines. Jesus' blood stabilizes ALL family units. Adoption must be near and dear to the heart of God. He planned it. He welcomes each of us into His family.

We pray this book can be a blessing to all whose lives have been privileged to be touched by the beauty of adoption. May it clear some of the confusion, misunderstandings, and worries surrounding the process of adoption. May it, as well, bring a clearer understanding of the truth and give a deeper perception of God's love.

"Thou shalt raise up the foundations of many generations" (Isaiah 58:12).   —Rhoda Bontrager

Foreword

From childhood, I have been inspired by parents willing to open their homes and their hearts to children not born to them, and to make these children a part of their family. My regard for them may be due in part to my own childhood. I do not remember my own mother, who died of childbirth complications when I was less than two years old. My baby brother survived and was soon adopted by a childless couple. When my father remarried, my stepmother accepted me as her own son when I needed a mother.

As the moral darkness around us intensifies, more and more innocent children are deprived the security of belonging to a two-parent family. As though that were not tragic enough, some would-be parents are being counseled not to pursue adoption because of the risks—the hassle of the adoption process, getting children with negative hereditary traits, or having ungrateful children trample their efforts underfoot. If potential parents are turned against adoption, who will provide homes for the many lonely, forsaken children needing to belong to a family?

What might counter the misgivings of the doubters? Knowing how we benefit from sharing experiences with those of similar interests, I began praying about the possibility of someone compiling a helpful book of adoption experiences.

Others supported the idea, but we did not find a capable, interested compiler. What a delight it was then, when Rhoda Bontrager called to inquire about Christian Light's interest in publishing the very kind of book we were needing. Having adopted four children themselves, and having assisted others with adoption details, has helped prepare

Thomas and Rhoda Bontrager for compiling the book you now hold in your hands.

While this book is about the experiences of others, rather than about how to be successful with adopting, it provides helpful tips and teaches valuable lessons.

You will read about couples who struggled to understand God's purpose for infertility. Lonely and distressed, they sought God's direction. As you read about the amazing ways God brought some of these families together, you will marvel at His unfailing love and concern for every child and every family.

Adoptive families are much like other families. To experience God's blessing, we must all order our families by His eternal principles. All children thrive in a climate of love, kindness, and affirmation, free from quarreling or harsh criticism. Adopted children, especially, thrive on unconditional love and acceptance. Parents are challenged to examine their motives for wanting to adopt. Is adoption for the benefit of the parents or the child?

My own life has been enriched by the privilege of meeting Thomas and Rhoda and their family, and by working together in the development of this book. I have been impressed with the concern of the various writers for children's feelings, and with the respect and appreciation they express for birthmothers who chose adoption rather than abortion. I have also been challenged with parents accepting adoption as God's plan for forming their family, not as a second-best solution to a problem.

While adoptive families are much like other families, they sometimes face thoughtless or uninformed responses from others. The following satire attempts to point out the impact of negative language in adoption:

Four Adoption Terms Defined

Natural child: any child who is not artificial.
Real parent: any parent who is not imaginary.
Your own child: any child who is not someone else's child.
Adopted child: a natural child, with a real parent, who is all my own.   —Rita Laws
<small>—From "Speaking Positively—An Information Sheet About Adoption Language" by Pat Johnston from Perspectives Press.</small>

May this book be a blessing to adoptive families and their relatives, to those contemplating adoption, and to many other readers. May it also be the means of helping sad, lonely children find secure, loving homes.

Adoption is a venture of faith—faith in God who specializes in forming happy families. "God places the solitary in families and gives the desolate a home in which to dwell" (Psalm 68:6, *The Amplified Bible*).

—Fred W. Miller
CLP Book and Tract Committee

What Is Adoption?

What is adoption? Adoption is voluntarily accepting a child into your family as your own. It involves a legal process which gives your adopted son or daughter identical rights and privileges as if they had been born to you. But most importantly, adoption is a matter of the heart. *"Lo, children are an heritage of the LORD"* (Psalm 127:3). That is true, whether children have come into our Christian homes through biological birth or adoption. Love is what makes a family.

Many couples contemplate adoption because they are physically unable to become birth parents. But adoption should not be pursued until a couple keenly senses God's leading and truly feels it is His best for them. Adoption should never feel "second best" to us. Adoption is the result of the wonderful love God showed to us when He chose us to be His sons and daughters. *We are not second-best, but have become His children and are joint-heirs with Jesus Christ* (Ephesians 1:3-6). Grafting usually improves a plant, so the love in adoption, along with biological bloodlines, can strengthen families and churches and help them thrive and grow. Adoption is a commitment of love. Traveling through infertility to a successful adoption is a long, difficult process. It is lonely; emotionally, physically, and financially draining; and lined with much loss and grief. But if it is God's will for you, and you allow God to carry you one step at a time, it is well worth it. Someday you will actually thank God for taking you down that path.

Most adoptions follow three steps: (1) the legal separation of the child from the birth parents, (2) transfer of custody, and (3) the transfer of parental rights and responsibilities to the adoptive parents. The actual adoption process itself has many variables that depend on whether you choose domestic or international adoptions, licensed agency, foster care, private or facilitator adoptions. All adoptions require a home study to begin with and an attorney to finalize.

A home study is a journey in itself! It will vary in cost from several hundred to several thousand dollars. It requires an autobiography from each spouse, fingerprints, police record checks, physicals, financial statements, reference letters, and sometimes, attending parenting classes. A resume type of letter to be shown to birthmothers also needs to be written. In this you need to include a description of your home, extended family, church, neighborhood, reasons for adopting, hobbies, educational goals, and parenting and discipline ideals.

Adoptions average from $10,000-20,000. The birthmother receives no money for relinquishing her rights, but she may receive some help with rent, medical expense, clothing, etc., related to her pregnancy. How much help she may receive varies greatly from state to state.

Before proceeding with an adoption, there are some important factors to consider. Both spouses must clearly feel the Lord's direction. Both must feel comfortable with building their family by adoption. Frequently the wife is ready to proceed before the husband because of her strong, God-given motherly instinct. The undertaking is much more successful if she can patiently submit and wait until her husband is also ready to move forward. It is good to ask counsel from parents and ministry. Quite often couples discover, to their dismay, that one set of parents is very supportive and the other side strongly anti-adoption. This complicates matters, but they need to make their own decision based on much prayer and seeking God's will. It is a real blessing when couples feel support from both extended families.

Couples dealing with infertility and endeavoring to discern God's will must realize adoption is not for everyone. A large variety of reasons could and should prevent a couple from pursuing adoption. A childless couple can be in the Lord's will and more effectively serve Him in some areas than a family would be able to.

As adoptive parents, we must be prepared to meet the needs of our children. All Christian parents need to provide their children with love and security. It is imperative that we are open and honest with them concerning their roots. In most cases the birthmother has not rejected her child, but put a lot of thought, love, and tears into her adoption plan. Approximately 90% of birthmothers change their mind shortly before or after the birth of the baby. They need much counseling "support." Choosing adoption is a very difficult decision for them to make. Only after seeing both the pain and the gratitude in a birthmother's face as she places her baby into your arms, can you humbly realize how great this gift really is. She is trusting you to provide the stability and love of a two-parent family. She is choosing you as a couple to parent this child. Being a parent is not merely being pregnant for nine months, but it is the nurturing, caring, teaching, and training that will continue the remainder of the child's life.

After you've decided this is really what you want to do, you can then weigh your options. There are several ways to proceed—through foster parenting, licensed agencies, networking, or private agencies.

Agencies typically have waiting lists of 6-8 years, but they do all the legwork for you. Whether networking or private, you hear about prospects, but you're on your own to follow through. Private is not for the fainthearted; you are more liable to "get burned." We worked with about 25 birthmothers and got three children.

You must remember, if God wants you to have a particular child, He will overcome all odds, and if not, even seemingly wide-open doors will close. Continually pray for His clear leading. Desperately wanting a baby in your arms sometimes distorts your vision. Decide if you are open to other nationalities, biracial, fetal alcohol syndrome, drug-affected infants, etc. Are you prepared to cope with special challenges? Cute babies do grow up. Also you must decide on how open an adoption you are comfortable with. An adoption support group is beneficial. Our group meets bimonthly. It gives us an opportunity to share encouragement, advice, and enjoy each other's positive experiences.

Our family was not born *to* us but *for* us. Like all children, they were born for a purpose. They may never do a special work as Moses and Esther did or as Samuel and the captive maiden who were not with their birthparents, but God has a plan and a special purpose for their lives. May God's blessing be on all adopted families, and we also wish His blessing and direction to those of you who are seriously contemplating adoption. The pain of empty arms goes to great physical and emotional depth. As you cry to the Lord, He will carry you through dealing with God-given desires for a family, difficult medical testing and treatment, and perhaps disparaging remarks from well-meaning people. He will strengthen you as you learn to rest and wait patiently to find His purpose for you as a couple.

One thing that often bothers us is when people say, "Oh, we just wouldn't adopt if it is so expensive and difficult." The same people work hard for other interests and readily borrow money for businesses, farms, vehicles, etc. These are temporal things. Why not borrow money for adoption? Our children are the only possessions we can take to heaven with us—what better eternal investment?

Thomas and Rhoda Bontrager

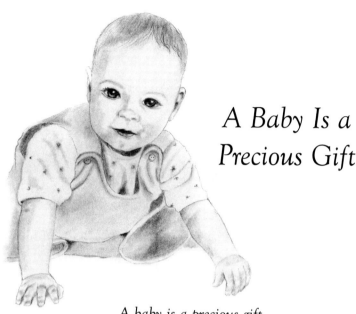

A Baby Is a Precious Gift

A baby is a precious gift,
A gift from God above,
And through the blessing of adoption
Is sent to earth to love.

A baby is a precious gift,
Unique in every way.
Created in God's image,
His glory to portray.

A baby is a precious gift,
The greatest gift on earth.
A chosen child and wanted one.
God's treasure of greatest worth!

Written by Mary Jane Proft.
Reprinted with permission of *Mary Sue Originals*.

Dean & Sheila Amstutz

Kyle — *September 4, 1998*

Kimberly — *January 17, 2000*

Kelsey — *February 7, 2001*

—Howe, Indiana

I held him close, so close to my heart! I could hear him breathing softly as his big eyes looked straight into mine. He was quiet and alert. I felt our hearts connect. He seemed to say, "Who are you, and where am I, and why is that light so bright?" He snuggled in closer as if to say, "I sorta like you!" *Well, guess what, Baby, I sorta like you too. I loved you way before I ever saw you . . . but do I dare breathe? Do I dare to even think this is true? Will you really be mine, all mine . . . forever?*

Dean and I had a wonderful marriage. We were happier than any two people could have possibly imagined to be. We did everything together. In our seven years of marriage, we'd ridden every wave together. We both came from very good homes. I was the oldest of five children and Dean the third of eight children. We both loved children. Everything was perfect except for one thing—a deep, dark, persistent ache that caused many, many tears, lots of questions and frustrations, and many tests and doctors. Then more questions and tears, frustrations, and denial, then doubting, anger, and sorrow. Oh, the emotions of seven years of infertility!

We had seen way too many doctors and nurses, if you asked us. At one point we had been told that, next to a

7

miracle, we would have no children. No children? Why?

After working through the doctoring and disappointments, we began to talk about adoption. Is that what God
had for us? I was ready and I was ready NOW! I was not afraid
of adoption. I had grown up with it. It was always a positive
experience. In fact, my best friend had been adopted. But
Dean was not ready. What he knew of adoption was pretty

Dean Amstutz family

much negative. It took him a while to accept the idea that there would probably be no biological children.

I am a person with little patience once I've made up my mind about something. It took a lot of patience and growing and learning to submit my timetable to my husband's. Finally I learned it. . . . I just began to pray that God would make him ready when, and if, we were supposed to proceed.

Not too long after, God answered, and Dean suggested I begin calling some agencies. I began to search for ways to begin. How do you begin an adoption journey anyway? Where do you even start?

The bits and pieces of information I had gathered over the years proved to be very helpful. Lutheran Social Services in Ft. Wayne, Indiana, helped us with our homestudy. But they wouldn't let us sign up for adoption through them because our wait would have been six to eight years. I'm glad now they were honest. We signed a two-year contract with A Silver Spoon Adoptions, a facilitator out of California. Only a couple weeks later we received our first birthmother call. That was the first of what would be many birthmother calls.

To make a long story short, twelve birthmothers later we had been matched twice, with both of them falling through. I was beginning to feel numb, not to mention frustrated. It was hard to hide the frustration and depression with every birthmother interview we endured. Our time was running out. We had been signed up for 15 months. The countdown was on to the end of our contract. What would happen then? Would we lose everything we had put into it? Would we never have a baby? Would adoption ever be a reality?

We prayed harder and sought advice from those who had been through this before. At this time we were given the best advice we had been told yet. "The squeaky wheel gets the attention." I started calling the agency every week, then

9

eventually every other day. The calls started coming.

I remember specifically how we had been to a trade show in Chicago with my sister, and we were on our way home. As we turned onto our road, the cell phone rang. It was our coordinator.

"Where are you?" she said, "I've got two calls waiting for you!"

We hurried home and started yet another birthmother interview. She was the sweetest one yet. She sounded so genuine. She had support from her parents and really cared about her baby and his parents-to-be. She was also young and horribly scared. And she chose US that very night! We were elated. This one felt different. Would it really happen? Would this baby be the one God had planned for us?

We were a bundle of nerves on our way to Iowa to meet the birthparents and birthgrandparents in person. They were as nervous as we were. We had such a good meeting! They were Christians. We had prayer several times before parting. It was so special. We took pictures together; we cried together. The birthmother handed me a note for the baby to keep and read when he was older. It was a true keepsake packed full of love. My heart went out to her. I watched as the tears flowed. There were so many emotions on her part too. I felt like we'd been friends forever. We'd both experienced so much.

The due date came and went. The doctor decided to induce labor, so off we went. As we entered the state of Iowa, I couldn't help but notice the state sign. It said, "IOWA—You make me smile." How true and fitting!

We met them in the waiting room at the hospital. The whole day was spent with the birthgrandparents in the waiting room. What loving people! They were so concerned about us and what we were experiencing too. How could they gather their emotions enough to worry about us? We had a lot in common. Even more so having Christ in common. They even thought far enough ahead to bring family photo albums for us to look through. Their family life and the life of the birthmom reminded us a lot of our own. It was really special, and I'm very glad we had that opportunity. We were all nervous wrecks. Would this actually happen? Would God actually bless us with this child?

Time stood still. The day seemed long. Everyone else's babies were being born. When would they announce ours? Finally at 9:00 p.m. Kyle Dean arrived. As birthgrandpa handed him to me, a certain awe swept over me. All the memories of the past one-and-a-half years flooded my mind, and now here I was, holding a precious baby that I hoped so much was mine.

The next week was full of ups and downs. Iowa has very strict laws on adoption due to the Baby Jessica case. It was interesting that we were dealing with the very same hospital. In a way it was a blessing. We felt confident that they were being extra cautious and yet were very accommodating. Finally the papers were signed and we went to our motel. We waited four more days before the signatures were recognized as valid.

In the meantime, the birthdad was struggling. In all our emotions, we couldn't help but hurt for him too. What a big decision to make, one that not only affects your life but someone else's life as well.

We prayed and prayed. We had several visitors from home which meant so much and helped to pass time. We were released from Iowa eight days later. Home never felt so good!

We settled into family life and enjoyed every second we could with Kyle. What a special little blessing!

When Kyle was 16 months old we began searching for an agency to help us add to our family. I contacted A Silver

11

Spoon again, not really sure if we were ready for another rollercoaster ride as big as the one we had just experienced. I called on Wednesday to inquire, and by Saturday they called us back wondering how serious we were. They had a baby due in two weeks. Were we interested? This was amazing! Could it actually be true? The adrenaline kicked in, and it was all we could do to keep up. We felt God was saying, "Would you just loosen up and follow Me?" Things were moving so fast we hardly knew if we were making proper decisions in the whole process or not.

Christmas Day found us flying to California. It was, oh, so hard to leave Kyle behind!

We met the birthmom at the doctor's office, then went to the hospital for an ultrasound. She had refused to allow them to do an ultrasound until the "parents" could be present for it. She made me feel so special. During the ultrasound we found out it was a little girl. Dean was elated. He was really hoping for a little girl. This was too special to be true. At one point during the ultrasound, the baby turned and looked directly at us. My heart stopped. She was so precious! As they handed me a picture I noticed her hands were folded as if she were praying. I burst into tears. What a perfect picture. God DOES have a plan for our lives, even from conception.

The birthmom requested that I be with her during the birth. She wanted me to be able to experience the birth of my daughter as much as possible. The doctor said the due date was off by 3-4 weeks and since she would need a C-section, we would have to wait for more tests to be done. We were disappointed. We elected to go home to wait since the doctor thought it might be at least a month away.

As we were flying home, despair hit. I had just seen the most precious little girl in the whole wide world, but it would be a miracle if we'd be returning for her. We kept

12

constant contact with the birthmom. She seemed to be genuine and pretty settled on her decision. Finally the call came that the baby was ready. We flew out the next day. We met birthmom at the hospital and, of course, the nerves were high again. I gave the birthmom a big hug and assured her I was as nervous as she was. We were in this together. I cared so much for her too, not just her baby, and I wanted her to know that.

They prepared her for surgery then offered me a chair beside her. I held her hand and rubbed her shoulders. I couldn't imagine the turmoil inside her. She was a strong woman—much stronger than I could've ever been. I admired her. I admire any birthmother who can be unselfish enough to lay down her desires for the best of her baby. I wanted her to know that I promised to love this little girl, not only for me, but for her too.

Kimberly Dawn was born kicking and screaming. She was a tiny little tyke, the size of a a doll and no bigger, so petite and healthy. Oh, the blessings God was bestowing on us!

The next morning we visited the birthmom. She was so scared we wouldn't show up. Her worst fear was that we'd leave and not come back. I wanted to say, "Not come back? Fly all the way to California twice for my baby girl and go home without her?" But I realized then that birthmoms have fears too. Big fears. My heart again went out to her and the deep hurt she was experiencing. If only I could comfort the emotions that were flooding her mind.

We flew home two weeks later. Kimberly was such a good baby; at times I wondered if she were an actual angel sent to us. We were so happy. It felt so good to be together as a family again.

A few months later God had another surprise for us. He decided another baby blessing would be just perfect for us. I found out I was pregnant. Pregnant? What?! A whole new set of emotions was in store for us! I hadn't realized until that moment how much I had actually worked through infertility, and how much I was okay with the way God was blessing us with a family. I had no desire to be pregnant. In fact, I didn't want to be at all. Oh, why was I struggling so? Yes, I wanted more children, and yes, coming from my own tummy would be so much easier, but couldn't I catch my breath a little first? My hands and arms were full, and now we would have three children in less than two-and-a-half years! Feelings of total inadequacy flooded over me. It was all so overwhelming. Worst of all, I couldn't understand why I was struggling so hard with the fact of being pregnant.

Well, God was patient, and He knew all things. Kelsey Brooke was born nine months later, and aside from being overwhelmed, we were happy. Another little girl just as cute and sweet as the first. They would grow up close and be best friends. Kyle was such a good big brother and very proud of his sisters.

I remember being ushered into my room after Kelsey's birth. My family had already arrived for a visit. They were so excited about yet another little one to cuddle. I remember thinking, *This seems so strange. You mean this is it? It's just that easy? No attorney telling me I'll have to wait three days to know if this baby is mine?* It didn't seem right. It was much too easy!

God is so good! We are delighted with our family. It's like the children say once in awhile, "Mom, I'm so glad we're a family!" That's exactly right! We wouldn't change any of it for the world. God is so divine, and the miracle behind each child's story is, oh, so precious.

Reflecting back over our experiences, one thought stands above the others. God is Almighty. He has a special purpose for everyone's life. His love is beyond our imagination. He is in control of everything. No matter how tensed up I get, He's still in control. So often I had to make a mental picture of me taking my hands and placing them behind my back, then letting God work out His will. When I did that, the miracles unfolded right before my eyes almost faster than I could watch! He is so very faithful. We are so blessed. We will never cease to praise Him—the Maker of all good things.

Now I think I'll go hug my children!

Joel & Rebecca Beachy

Michael — *November 14, 1996*

Jonathan — *February 13, 2000*

Elizabeth — *June 27, 2001*

Peter — *May 19, 2002*

Hannah — *November 19, 2002*

—Traverse City, Michigan

We, Joel and Rebecca Beachy, were born and raised in northern Indiana and were married in May 1992. After spending a year and a half in Florida with Choice Books, we chose to make our home in Traverse City, Michigan. We are members of the Traverse Bay Mennonite Church, which is part of the Midwest Fellowship. Joel works for Golden Rule Construction as a finish carpenter.

As young couples do, we expected God to give us children biologically and in our timing. But after our move to Michigan and still no children, we began to experience hurt, and asked God why we weren't finding our fulfillment. God's timing is best, and His ways are not our ways.

The reality of infertility caused us to look at other possibilities for having children. Joel's employer shared how they had enjoyed being foster parents, and we began thinking along that route. We had several meetings with a local foster care agency, but it looked too heartbreaking to give a child back after being with us for a while. Today we understand it

17

to mean we weren't ready. We still had our focus on ourselves rather than on helping a child, as foster parents need
to. God used His own timing. In December of 1995 the foster care agency called to see if we would reconsider becoming foster parents, stating they needed more homes to parent infants and small toddlers. God repeatedly opened
doors, and we moved through. We became licensed foster
parents in May of 1996, just before our fourth anniversary.

Our oldest son, Michael, was the first child placed with
us. He was 3½ weeks old when he came in December of
1996. We definitely were ready to hear a baby's cry in our
home! Michael was with us two months when it was decided

Joel Beachy family

in court that he would not be returned to his birthparents. When a foster child is not able to be reunited with his or her biological parents and no other family member, such as a grandparent, aunt, or uncle, is interested in or accepted by court to adopt the child, then foster parents usually have first chance to adopt. We were privileged to adopt Michael. His adoption was done in May of 1997, when he was six months old.

We had ten foster children come and go before Jonathan, our second child, came. He was born in February of 2000, and came to stay with us when he was 2½ weeks old. He was close to a year old when the court decided he would not be reunited with his biological parents, and we were excited to adopt another child. His adoption was completed when he was 15 months old.

We then had two other foster children here for a short while, and after those cases, we were asked to take Elizabeth, our third child. Elizabeth was born in June of 2001 and was placed with us when she was six weeks old. When she was 10½ months old, her biological brother, Peter, who was born in May, came to us right from the hospital. While their cases (which were handled separately) were pending, we were told that Jonathan's biological sister, Hannah, was born and needed a home. With Peter only six months old at the time, it seemed overwhelming. Our hearts said yes, but our hands were so full. We sought counsel from our church family and decided to take her. So Hannah came in November 2002, two days after she was born.

Elizabeth's case moved into the adoption process next. She was 19 months old when her adoption was signed in January 2003. Several months later we were happy to learn we could adopt a second girl. Hannah's adoption took place in March, when she was only four months old. Then Peter was adopted in March 2003, when he was 10 months old.

All of our adoptions were handled in the adoption department of our foster care agency, and were signed by our judge here in Traverse City. We feel blessed to be able to be adoptive parents, and hope to pass that excitement to our children. Our goal is to show them who Jesus is.

An Adoption Prayer

Not flesh of my flesh
Nor bone of my bones
But still miraculously my own—
Never forget for a single minute
You didn't grow under my heart
But in it.

—Author Unknown

3

Phillip & Connie Bear

Jeremy Lee — *April 23, 1983*

Janelle Marie — *September 20, 1988*

Robert Eugene — *December 29, 1990*

Diana Rose — *April 14, 1995*

Carmen Alisa — *April 16, 1998*

—Parsonsburg, Maryland

Before I begin our adoption stories, I'll first give a brief introduction to our family. We are Phillip and Connie Bear of Parsonsburg, Maryland. The Lord has blessed us with five children—two biological and three through adoption. Their ages now are as follows: Jeremy (20), Janelle (14), Bobby (12), Diana (8), and Carmen (5). We attend the Salisbury Mennonite Church near Salisbury, MD. Phil and his brothers worked together in construction until a couple of years ago when they bought a garage door business. Phil now works in the office there and Jeremy has been doing installation.

Like many other couples, infertility was probably a key issue in our decision to adopt. Phil and I were married June 12, 1982, and the following year on April 23, Jeremy Lee joined our family. When Jeremy was about a year and a half, I had to have emergency surgery for ovarian cysts and a few days later miscarried. That surgery resulted in painful adhesions, which required more surgery. It was then that we were given the heartbreaking news that there was almost no chance of having any more children. Around that time we started doing foster care, which we continued for eight years. We hoped to adopt if a child became available, but did not realize that we should have gotten dual licensing for foster care and adoption if we wanted to have a pre-adopt child placed with us. We cannot remember that there was anything special leading to a decision to adopt. We both loved children and knew it did not matter how they came. At a time when our struggle with infertility was the most severe, God led me to the verse in Psalm 113:9, "He maketh the barren woman to keep house, and to be a joyful mother of children." It was like a special promise from the Lord that He did have a joyful work for me as a mother, whether it was biological, adopted, or foster children. Doing foster care

Phillip Bear family

gave us a real sense of fulfillment during our years of waiting for a baby.

In the fall of 1985 or early 1986 we started actively pursuing adoption. We chose to work with Bethany Christian Services. Their main office is in Michigan, with branch offices in other states. We worked with the branch that was in Annapolis, Maryland, at that time. We felt they would be more understanding of our beliefs and goals for our children. Their waiting list was also shorter. We really enjoyed working with them during the homestudy and attending the required classes, etc. By the spring of 1988 we were third on the waiting list (they were placing an average of one baby a month) and getting very excited about soon getting a baby, when we realized that contrary to what the doctors thought possible, we were going to have another biological child! Bethany's policy is not to place healthy babies in homes where there are already two children. But they kept us on the waiting list until Janelle Marie was born on September 20, 1988.

Robert Eugene (Bobby) was born on December 29, 1990, and came to us at three months old as a foster child. He had just been released from the hospital after having hemorrhaging in the brain from abuse for the second time. For about a year-and-a-half, Social Services continued to work with the birthparents in hopes of reuniting the family. Social Services asked us if we would be willing to have the birthparents come out to our home twice a week to try to teach them how to care for Bobby. After that, Social Services started visits in the birthparents' home. About every six months, Bobby's case went back to court, and each time the social workers felt that he should not go back home, but they did not have enough evidence to keep him in their care. But each time something came up at the hearing to keep him in care longer. After two other siblings were abused,

23

Social Services began plans to terminate parental rights. When they told us they would have a hard time finding a home for Bobby because of his significant developmental delay, we assured them that Bobby already had a home. We did have concerns about the future of raising a mentally challenged child, but felt God had placed him in our home and our lives, and if He worked out the adoption details, we should go ahead.

Knowing the birthfather's anger and that he knew where we lived made us uneasy, but that was taken care of. When the birthparents realized things were not working out for them, they requested that we adopt Bobby and that Phil's brother and wife (where the siblings had been placed) adopt the girls. We had agreed to go to Belize for a two-year term, but the social workers did not think they could have the rights terminated and an adoption finalized by the time we needed to leave. We knew if God wanted us to have Bobby, He could take care of that problem too. To the social workers' amazement, the adoption was completed and Bobby had his passport within two months of beginning the process. We were glad to have those two years of uncertainty behind us and know that Bobby was ours.

Bobby's birthfather felt it was best that he stay out of the children's lives, and we have not seen him since the adoption. We occasionally see the birthmother in town and try to make yearly visits to her mother's home for the family to see Bobby. She knows she is unable to care for the children and is satisfied with the situation.

In March of 1993 we moved to Belize to work with the Hummingbird Mission. That summer someone told us about a mother who was looking for someone to adopt her five-week-old baby boy. We contacted her, and she decided to place her baby in our home. What a joy little Jared was! The whole family was soon very attached to him and eagerly

24

awaited the time we would know he was ours. Jared had been with us a month when we met with the birthmother to sign the preliminary adoption papers. What a relief to have that hurdle behind us! But that joy was short-lived. Early the next morning, when the family was happily playing with Jared on the bed, the bus stopped outside our house. It was the birthmother coming to ask if we would please consider giving him back to her. Once she had signed the papers, she realized she just could not go through with giving him up. It was a heartbroken family that packed up his things that morning and turned our precious baby back over to his birthmother. We knew our main concern had to be for her soul and our witness in the community, and we wanted to show a Christlike response. We knew the birthmother could not afford Jared's formula, and yet she was a very good mother, so we continued to supply his formula. We also baby-sat for him while she worked. We still have a good relationship with the family and visit Jared when we are in Belize.

After that experience, we felt as though we could never pursue adoption again. But after returning to Belize from furlough in 1995, we were told that an acquaintance in the next village (where Phil sold milk) was caring for her two-month-old granddaughter and felt she was too old to meet her needs adequately. She had said that when Mr. Felipe's family came home, she was going to give the baby to them. We felt we could not handle another disappointment, so did not want to pursue it. But at the grandmother's request, Phil did go for a visit. She told him she wanted us to have the baby, but she first wanted to inform the mother, whose whereabouts were unknown.

A few days later the grandmother was requesting that I also go to see the baby. The memories of being hurt the other time and knowing the birthmother had still not been located, made me very reluctant to get involved. Phil's warning to "hang on to your heart if you do go" and knowing the baby had already taken his heart, made me even more afraid of getting hurt again. Struggling with the fear of being disappointed again, we asked the Lord, that if it was His will that we have the baby, that the grandmother would change her mind about having to find the mother and would send the baby home with us that day. When we arrived at their house, she again confirmed her intention to contact her daughter before she gave us the baby. Then she had someone bring the baby to me. When they put Diana in my arms, she looked up at me with her big eyes and immediately began cooing and cooing through big smiles! The grandmother was so astonished. She said Diana had never acted like that for anyone before. She was soon packing up Diana's clothes and birthpapers and telling us to take her with us right away! How thankful we were that God so compassionately looked on our emotional needs at that time. Diana Rose was born April 14, 1995, and came home to live with us two-and-one-half months later on July 6.

Belizean law allows a relative to sign adoption papers when a child has been abandoned by a parent, so Diana's grandmother was able to do this. We found a good lawyer in Belize City, who had the adoption finalized by October 17, 1995.

We have felt comfortable with a "grandparent" relationship with Diana's birth family. There was a time when her grandmother began coming up during church services and taking her from my arms to take her to the back and play with her. We began to feel the need of more "space" between us. We came back to the States in April 1996 for eleven months, then returned to Belize to serve in the Orange Walk area. We have continued to have a good relationship with Diana's grandparents and feel as though it has been a positive experience for all of us.

In February 1998 we received a letter from a young woman who had stayed with us for a few days about three years earlier when there had been conflict in her home. Her baby was due in about six weeks, and since her husband had left her, she felt unable to care for another child. She wanted her child in a Christian home and was requesting that we adopt him/her. My first impulse was to quickly send a letter back with the one who had brought her letter to us, saying that we would certainly want to adopt the baby. Phil, however, wisely decided that we would first spend a couple of weeks praying and asking advice. We made a trip to where some of the relatives lived and talked to the grandfather, uncle, and aunt of the baby to see how they felt about the situation. They were very supportive of us taking the baby. Since we were also sensing the Lord's leading to go ahead through positive feedback from our families and other mission workers, we wrote to the birthmother of our desire to adopt the baby. The next few weeks were filled with the excitement of preparation for the coming baby and dread that the mother would change her mind. She had requested that she could come stay with us for two weeks prior to the due date. Those were very emotional and stressful days for all of us, but a time we can now look back to as a blessing. We saw the love she had for her baby and the pain she was experiencing in giving it up. We assured her of our love and support, even if she decided to change her mind and keep the baby, though our hearts were pleading that it would not be so.

The time finally arrived to go to the hospital. Our little Carmen Alisa was born in the early morning of April 16, 1998. Since the birthmother had decided it was best for her not to see the baby after birth, I was allowed to stay at the hospital to care for Carmen until we took her home the next day.

The time of parting with the birthmother was another very difficult time. How can you adequately thank someone for the gift of her child, especially after seeing the pain it has cost her? We could only cling to each other and cry—two mother-hearts mingling their joy, sorrow, and love for this child.

We used the same lawyer in Belize City that we had used for Diana's adoption. By the time Carmen was three months old the adoption was finalized.

Because of health problems, we had to return to the States when Carmen was about two-and-one-half months old. So far we have returned to Belize every year to visit or fill in for furloughs, etc., and we always visit Diana and Carmen's families. The families have always expressed their gratitude that we have the girls and that we allow them to be involved in their lives.

Many of the challenges we face in raising children are not unique to adopted children. Our biological children also face struggles, and we need the same commitment to parenting both. We can honestly say we have felt no difference in our relationship to our biological or adopted children. However, some children do come to us with unique problems caused by abuse, neglect, or prenatal alcohol and drug exposure. In adoption classes, we were told that no matter how young a child was when he was adopted, he will at some time face a grieving for the family he lost. We need to be prepared for that time and not feel threatened by it.

It is important that our attitudes toward the birthparents are respectful and appreciative, even though sometimes we cannot understand the choices they have made. The children need to know there was love behind the decision to let them go. Birth families are very important people in their lives and whether we choose to allow them to be involved in the lives of our children or feel it is best to wait until they

28

are older, we will all benefit from a proper attitude. We have chosen to have an open relationship with our children's birth families, probably in part because of having a relationship with them before the adoption. We have felt it best to keep the contact limited, usually visiting and/or sending pictures once a year. We do not refer to their birthmothers as their mothers, but by name as any other friend. The girls' Hispanic grandparents are called Abuelo and Abuela to cause less confusion.

Opinions of our extended families and the support of the church family are very important in adoptions. Children can quickly detect if they are not accepted or treated equally. But we cannot expect everyone to feel immediately as we do about our adoption experience. The Lord has not prepared their hearts in the same way He has ours, and they may need more time for bonding. We have been blessed with family and friends supportive of our adoptions. Having other adopted children in our family and church is also a blessing for us. We have probably had more negative responses when facing problems with our special needs child. We have had suggestions to send him back or heard that it is our problem because we accepted him. Probably the less we make an issue out of responses that we take as negative, the less they will affect our children. Not everyone will understand that our love and commitment to this child is the same as to a birthchild. Sometimes it's just as hard to know how to handle the comments of people we meet. We often hear, "They are so lucky to be with you!" No, we are so blessed. It is obvious to everyone that our two Hispanic children are adopted. A question we often face is, "Are they sisters?" Although we know what people mean, we do not want the girls to feel unsettled. We usually answer with, "Yes, they are sisters, but not biological." Another question is, "Do you have any children of your own?" Our favorite answer to that was one

29

Diana gave a couple of years ago when just two of the children were with me. She quickly replied to the woman who asked, "Yes, we *all* are and we have three more at home!" We like to assure people that we have *five* children of our own—all graciously given to us by God in different ways.

4

Phil & Jan Beiler

Conrad Benjamin — *March 24, 1983*

Harlan Dale — *September 1, 1985*

Deryk Lane — *December 6, 1987*

Francie Janelle — *September 7, 1988*

Chadwin Jacob — *January 4, 1995*

Micah Wayne — *March 20, 1997*

Donovan Jose — *November 14, 2001*

Merideth Fern — *December 3, 2001*

—Pantego, North Carolina

I sit down at the computer to write our adoption story in a rare, quiet moment. The telephone rings. While I'm talking on the phone I wash a few dishes, which reminds me, I want to get pork chops out of the freezer for supper. Once I'm in the utility room, I see the washer is full of water, and I forgot to put the towels in. I head for the bathroom to get the towels and hear Merideth cry. I take her out of her crib and smell a peculiar odor. After I change her, I take her to the kitchen for a snack, and I see Micah has rooted up the junk drawer and left a pile of stuff on the floor. I call him to come pick it up and start wiping off the countertop. Donovan comes toddling into the house behind Micah with two green trails between his nose and his upper lip. All of a sudden I remember the dirty towels. . . . And now I'm back at the computer with Merideth on my lap trying to bang on the keyboard and Micah holding his new preschool math book between me and the screen saying, "Do this . . . do this . . ."

Nineteen years ago I would have loved to preview this scene, chaotic as it is—back when the house was silent except for the noise the two of us generated. Back when we called one adoption agency after another and always heard the same answer although the reasons differed. "I'm sorry, we can't help you . . ." Either the cost was prohibitive, I was too young, or we hadn't been married long enough. I remember plunking the receiver down on the cradle of the desk phone, burying my head in my arms and sobbing after another dead-end call. "Oh, Lord," I cried. "Isn't there a way for us somehow to adopt a child?"

I battled resentment against ladies whose lives seemed to

Phil Beiler family

go as planned, with one doll-faced child carefully spaced after an equally attractive other.

One day my mother called and said she ran across an article in *The Budget* about someone who had adopted from Guaimaca, Honduras. If one child had been adopted there, might there be others available? I didn't even know where Honduras was, so I got out the map and pored over it until I found it tucked away in Central America, next to Guatemala.

I wrote to the editor of *The Budget* for the mailing address of the Honduras scribe. When it came, I jotted a letter of inquiry southward. Two weeks later I found an airmail envelope in our box. With shaking fingers I tore it open. *Yes, we have children available to adopt,* Laura Miller had written. And then, how my heart leapt. *Right now we have more children than parents who are waiting.*

A bold idea gripped us. "If that's the case," we reasoned, "we may as well ask for two as for one."

The postal service didn't recognize the urgency of our letter, and it took four whole weeks until they delivered the news that we could indeed adopt two children from the children's home. They gave us several names and brief descriptions to choose from.

Two-and-one-half-year-old Joshua (Conrad), stepped off the page at us as well as tiny baby Jason (Harlan). The very next letter from Laura contained a picture of Conrad, wearing a little brown pair of homemade pants, sitting in the grass beside an infant seat where a fat little Harlan squinted into the sun. My heart yearned for them.

We went right to work, finding out what was involved in an adoption. We called agencies, wrote letters to the state department of human resources, and visited people who had adopted from Honduras. We wandered through the maze of immigration applications and home study evaluations. We collected references, bank statements, property deed, criminal record check, and more. We carried them from clerk of court to state department to Honduran consulate for authentication. Every time we ran into an obstacle, the Lord somehow showed us a bridge over it, a tunnel under it, or a detour around it.

We worked directly with the lawyer in Honduras, as in a private adoption. Since he spoke very little English, I relied heavily on my Spanish-speaking sister-in-law, Marie, to make telephone connections. While she asked the questions I had scrawled on paper, I waited breathlessly in the background for updates.

The day finally came when we would meet our little boys in person. When we arrived at the children's home, Conrad was already in his pajamas. I sat beside him on the couch and showed him pictures from a Bible story book. His black hair shone in the lamp light, and I wanted to wrap my arms around his thin frame and kiss him, but I worried about coming on too strong. Harlan lived in another house on the orphanage grounds with Ruth Wagler, who is a nurse. We ate supper with her, and I learned how to eat slippery noodles while holding an eight-month-old baby who kept grabbing for my spoon. Harlan smiled easily and seemed perfectly contented. We had merely traveled to Honduras to sign papers, not finish the adoption. All too soon we had to board our plane and leave the boys behind. Now that we had become acquainted with our children we could hardly wait to bring them home. While we knew they were receiving excellent care at the Home, *I* wanted to be the one to give them their baths and read their nighttime stories. *We* wanted to hear Conrad's bedtime prayers and watch Harlan pull himself up at the couch and take his first wobbly steps.

Three months later, we packed our bags again. This time we had an extra suitcase filled with little clothes and shoes, a few toys, and a lot of love. Our lawyer, Mario Idiaquez told us to plan to stay two to four weeks. We optimistically figured it shouldn't take more than two.

We moved into the clinic with Ruth. As a missionary nurse, she had plenty to do, so we quickly settled into a comfortable rhythm where I did most of the housework and she took care of a foster baby and all the community folks who happened by with ailments. The boys' personalities took shape as we learned to know them. Conrad's imagination delighted us. He loved to play that the porch swing was an airplane, and we were flying to the States. When his airplane broke down, he crawled under it and fixed it with a gadget from the kitchen, or whatever. Harlan crawled around on his daily tour, slopping in the water bucket, pulling things off the nightstand in the bedroom and unwinding toilet paper.

One week followed another and we couldn't tell what, if anything, was happening with the adoptions. Phil made numerous trips to Tegucigalpa, the capital city. Sometimes the boys and I went with him. We learned which buses to take, which restaurants to patronize, and which restrooms to avoid. We spent countless hours in the dark little cubicle of Mario's waiting room. He was either out on business, out to lunch, or at the court. Many times we were invited to "Come back at two o'clock," or "Come back on Thursday." We whiled away time in Central Park, listening to enthusiastic evangelists thunder at the milling crowds, watching a snake handler, or just resting on a bench, deflecting beggars and listening to salesmen yelling their wares. Sometimes we went to the Communications building and called home.

The two weeks stretched into three, then four. The missionaries at the children's home included us in their lives, often inviting us for meals or arranging their schedules to take us into town so that we could avoid the bus hassle.

35

Finally, after fifteen weeks, the adoption was complete. It seemed like there should be whistles blowing and cymbals clanging to help celebrate as we mounted the steps of the aircraft that would bear us home.

Home with our boys! Our little house rang with the boys' laughter and bristled with their spats. Toys littered the floor and smudges appeared on windows, walls, and doors. It was what we had longed for!

About a year after the adoption was finished, the administrator of the children's home, Eli Hershberger, called and wondered if we would be interested in a set of twin boys. We became all excited about it, picked out names, and imagined what it would be like to have four boys so close together in age.

By the time we found out the twins wouldn't be adoptable, we were geared to expand our family. We asked if there were any other children available, and that is how we started the adoption of nine-month-old Deryk and two-day-old Francie.

It took six months before we could bring the babies home. Dark-eyed Deryk took an instant dislike to most men, and his daddy was no exception. When Phil came home from work and the other children eagerly greeted him at the door, Deryk fled up the stairs. If Phil held him, he'd dissolve into tears. Phil patiently worked to win him over. One day when Phil brought a snack home for the children in a paper bag, he noticed how attentive Deryk became when the paper rustled. He invented a little routine of bringing something home in a paper bag for Deryk every evening after work. It didn't take long until the little fellow was completely won over and joined the other children in welcome even when no bags were in sight.

Francie, with her long dark lashes and curly hair, lapped up attention from everyone. Weeks passed before I had the satisfaction of her actually showing a preference for me as her mother.

The children seemed to adjust well to our home and community. The boys spent countless hours exploring the swamp behind our house or fishing for crayfish and other slimy things from our ditch.

Several busy years passed before the craving for another baby hit us. By this time the country of Honduras no longer processed adoptions, and we didn't know what alternatives there were. I started the round of calling agencies again, and this time I heard things like, "You already have four children. We give first opportunity to those who are still waiting for a child."

We investigated private adoptions and interstate adoptions, but everything seemed to come to a dead end. Several times we learned of babies here or there, and after we had gotten all excited about them, the case would disintegrate. Once we thought we were in line to get my cousin's two little girls, but before anything materialized, she reformed enough to keep them.

Then one day, Marie told me about a rumor she'd heard from the Mexicans in our area. "A girl is going to have a baby, and she says she can't keep it. The problem is, she's moved and no one seems to know where. Let's pray that something will come of it."

Since Marie's prayers usually get answers, it should have come as no surprise when she arrived at my door sometime later flagging a yellow scrap of paper. "I have her address," she said triumphantly.

Of course, that didn't mean the lady would be inclined to give her baby to us. Marie contacted her, and after we had nearly given up hope, she finally sent word that she would like for us to have her baby.

We nervously waited the three remaining weeks until her

due date. Would she change her mind? I wanted to rip a page off the calendar to make time go faster. How could we endure the suspense any longer? I washed windows and cleaned out the attic.

Then finally, baby Chad arrived, all ten pounds of him. Our family gathered around the nursery window and wondered if it could be true!

Chad won our hearts from the beginning. Every little wiggle and smile indicated his exceptional genius. At his first little squeak in the morning, the children fought to get him out of his cradle.

In order to finish the adoption, we either needed the father's signature or proof of his negligence, in order to terminate parental rights. Chad's mother warned against finding him. "He is a bad man," she repeated. "He will cause trouble."

Our lawyer tried to locate him, but after several attempts gave up. "We'll have to advertise in the newspaper for thirty days," he said. "I don't think it will be a problem. He has not shown interest in the child up until now. There's a good chance he won't even see the ad."

On the twentieth day of the advertisement, I was carrying a stack of folded clothes into the bedroom when the phone rang. I glanced at the clock on the nightstand and thought, *Good, it's after five, it won't be the lawyer.*

But it *was* the lawyer. "I'm sorry, but I have bad news for you." My heart plummeted. "Chad's father called today. He is very upset and says he is going to hire a lawyer and get the baby back. I almost get the feeling he is retaliating at the embarrassment of having his name publicized in connection with giving a child away."

How could it be God's will for our precious son to be raised by that ungodly man? But even as I questioned, I knew things like that have happened plenty of times and God permits it. We

38

don't have to understand why.

We wanted to cuddle Chad every minute and absorb all the details of every precious bit of him. We knew if we had to give him up, our prayers would follow him until the day we died. *Maybe that is why God gave him to us for awhile,* I thought. *Otherwise he wouldn't have had anyone to pray for him.*

Chad's father was given an additional thirty days to prepare his defense. A whole month! It loomed ahead like a mountain. In the meantime, we prayed incessantly. Word of our crises spread, and soon the phone rang again and again as our friends called to assure us of their prayers. A warm blanket of love and support enveloped us. How comforting to cast ourselves on the mercy of our heavenly Father and know nothing can happen He does not allow.

One snail-paced day after another crept by. We didn't hear anything more from the father, but we didn't know if that was good or bad.

And then it was court day. What would this day bring forth? Would Chad's father be present with a silver-tongued lawyer? Would he have a dozen witnesses in tow to vouch for his sterling character? Would this be our last morning with Chad as our son? We chose to leave Chad behind. If the man saw what a handsome son he had produced, he would be sure to raise a ruckus. I bathed Chad tenderly and crushed him in a last embrace as we deposited him with my niece.

It took a moment for our eyes to adjust to the dark interior of the courthouse. The lawyer met with us for a few words. A crowd of people surged around the courtroom doors. I scanned faces. There were white people and black people. My heart gave a little leap. At least there weren't any Hispanic people in the entryway. Neither were there any inside the courtroom. Were they still coming? Every time the double doors opened I glanced anxiously toward them.

I strained to hear footsteps. Every nerve in my body seemed on guard.

Voices echoed off the high, embossed metal ceiling. Four long windows looked out onto the dingy street below. The room smelled like old wood.

The judge heard one case after another. People came and went. The clock ticked on. The courtroom cleared. Finally our case was the only one left to be heard. Chad's father had not shown up.

We visited briefly with the lawyer after the judge terminated the father's parental rights. "I don't understand why the man stayed away after the fuss he made," the lawyer commented.

But we understood. We knew God intervened.

For years Francie prayed for a sister. She included it in every mealtime prayer she prayed and every night when she went to bed. What a disappointment when Chad turned out to be a boy. I tried to comfort her by saying, "Well, now maybe we'll get to adopt again." Only we weren't sure where to start. After a few more false tries and dashed hopes, we learned about a lawyer from Costa Rica. We would basically use the same system we used in Honduras, doing our own footwork. And so we dumped ourselves back into the adoption maze.

Although Micah was due in January, he was not born until March. I called the translator nearly every week. We began to wonder how many times Virginia must be changing mothers on us. Had we invested money in a fraudulent scheme? We called one of the brethren in Costa Rica and asked if he knew anything about a lawyer named Virginia _____ . He said they have used her occasionally, and he thinks she's okay.

A few days later Glen Bontrager called from Costa Rica. He said they understand we are working on an adoption, and they would be glad to do foster care for us if we didn't have other plans. We gratefully accepted their offer, and when the baby finally arrived on March 20, he was taken from the hospital to their mountain home. Micah's foster mother, Margaret, kindly sent pictures and letters to introduce him to us.

Glens had also applied to adopt a child through Virginia. One of their daughters had died a few years before, and it was evident they had the same insatiable appetite for children we had. They showered Micah with their love, and he grew and prospered.

When Micah was three months old, we traveled to Costa Rica for the first signing. Glen and Margaret met us at the airport and took us to their home. We marveled at their gracious hospitality when we saw how lavishly they loved Micah. I knew myself well enough to know that if I had to lodge someone who would take my baby away, I would want to give them a lumpy mattress to sleep on and unseasoned beans three meals a day.

Micah was a chubby little fellow with dark, slanty eyes and long lashes. He allowed us to hold him but he seemed to regard us with suspicion as if he sensed our mission. I enjoyed holding him, even though he felt like someone else's child. In all of our other adoptions, I knew our children were better off to come with us than stay where they were. With Micah, I had the sneaking suspicion we'd have a hard time being better parents than Glens.

We enjoyed the lush wildflowers along the mountainous highways in Costa Rica. I thought I had never seen such large impatiens. From Glen's living room window we caught glimpses of the coastline and often a rainbow appeared through the mists. Coffee plantations thrived nearby. On Sunday we attended the Spanish service in the little village of Bijagua and ate lunch with Levi Friesens.

41

We brought lots of pictures and stories home to share with our other children. I began praying with renewed zeal for the Lord to send Glens a baby before it came time for us to take Micah. The time for our return grew closer and closer.

Finally we had the appointment for Micah's passport. The adoption was all but done. Glens still didn't have a baby. We packed our suitcases with a mixture of joy and heaviness.

Micah was even cuter than I remembered. He had learned to sit and was very active. Glens took us to the city of San Jose to finish our business. We had to stay overnight so they helped us engage a nice hotel and they headed home, without Micah. I can still see them walking out across Central Park.

We enjoyed learning to know Micah. We laid him on the bed and he seemed glad to be turned loose. He wiggled and rolled and Phil took pictures. I felt like a little girl playing doll as I bathed and dressed him to go out for supper that evening.

Glen's three children were especially happy to welcome Micah home when we returned from the city. Lorna, Margaret's sister who lived with them, set him on a blanket in the yard and took pictures of him.

At family worship, the last morning we were in Costa Rica, Glen prayed a special blessing on Micah as he adjusted to his new home and family. He borrowed a vehicle from a neighbor so there would be enough room for all of their family to go with us to the airport.

We stopped beside a waterfall on the way to the city and Glen asked Phil to take one last family picture of them with Micah. A choky feeling welled up inside me as they gathered in front of the rocks, holding Micah and smiling bravely.

When we landed in Norfolk, Va., Phil's mother and sister

were there to meet us with all our children. The children took turns welcoming their new brother. Even Francie thought a baby boy was better than no baby at all. Chad did not seem especially impressed, and in the days that followed, when Micah cried too much he'd say, "I wish you would send him back to Glen and Margaret on the airplane."

Six children seemed like a nice family, but Francie was still praying for another sister. We thought we'd try one more time to adopt a little girl, but we weren't sure when or where. Glens were having such a time with Virginia, we weren't sure we wanted to risk working with her again.

Then, of course, there was the money issue. In the next several years we had a fairly major hospital expense, and when the motor went bad on our aging van we decided to replace the whole vehicle.

We may have given up the idea of another adoption if Chad's mother hadn't called Marie and said she knew of another lady who wanted to give up her child. The sonogram showed a baby girl. It seemed too good to be true—and it was.

By the time we discovered the mother had moved off to California, and we weren't going to get her child, we also discovered we weren't ready to call our family complete.

We contacted Carolina Adoption Services, the agency who did our home study for Micah, since they had a program out of Guatemala that looked good to us. Soon after we submitted our dossier, our adoption coordinator called. "Jan, we have a set of twins in Guatemala. I don't have many details yet, but I do know one is a girl and the other is a boy. Would you be interested?"

Would we be interested?! I felt at that moment like all I'd ever wanted was a set of twins. The first pictures arrived about a week after we gave our answer. Kaitlyn was beautiful—smooth pink skin that looked velvety to the touch, perfectly arched eyebrows over liquid, black eyes, a dainty mouth, and the most exquisite little nose. Black, gossamer-like hair framed her oval face.

"Isn't she lovely?" we exclaimed.

Kaleb peered up at us through squinty black eyes, one hand upraised as if in protest. His puckered lips with milky residue clinging to the edges looked like someone had popped a bottle out just long enough to snap the picture. His black hair stood up in little tufts around his scrunched-up face. A faint dimple was etched on one cheek. My heart stirred within me. *He looks like he needs me,* I thought.

"Isn't he precious?" we said.

Since an adoption from Guatemala normally takes five to seven months, we counted up the months until we could reasonably expect to bring the twins home. We posted their pictures on the refrigerator for everyone to see. The older boys, who at first weren't too sure about the idea, began to look forward to learning to know the two babies. Every night when I tucked the younger children into bed we prayed for Kaleb and Kaitlyn. Alone in her double bed, twelve-year-old Francie couldn't wait for a sister to snuggle with.

Two months passed. At the end of each month when the twins' foster mother took them to the doctor for check-ups, the doctor snapped their pictures and e-mailed them to our coordinator, Carl Hocke. Carl, in turn, e-mailed them to us. As each month drew to a close, we hung around the computer. Every time a nearly life-sized baby filled the screen our love for them grew. By now Kaleb's face had filled out, and he took on a robust, eager look. The doctor reported good health, normal development, and lusty appetites.

One morning in early June after the morning hustle of getting Phil and the boys off to work, I sat down with a bowl of Raisin Nut Bran and a book. The phone rang.

"Jan. This is Carl. I have bad news." Fear clutched at my heart. *Now what?* I went into my room, lay across the bed, and looked out the window as Carl explained the news. Outside rain poured from soggy, gray clouds.

Kaleb and Kaitlyn's mother had been killed by a mob. The adoption could not proceed until someone else became legally responsible to sign for them. Although the grandparents would be the likely candidates for this, they were separated from each other and the grandmother had been estranged from her daughter, the twins' mother. Would she even cooperate? Things didn't sound good.

Our family and friends began to pray more earnestly than ever.

A few days later Carl called again. "Your prayers must be doing some good," he said. The grandmother had left her husband years ago when her children were small. The grandfather had been given custody way back then, and so now he could go ahead with becoming the legal representative for the babies whether the grandmother cooperated or not. He was perfectly willing to do so and had already collected the necessary documents and presented them to the lawyer.

"Isn't God good!" we rejoiced.

We were still in for a long wait because the *tutela,* or guardianship, the grandfather needed could take anywhere from four to six months to acquire. And after that the whole long adoption process would start again. *How old is the grandfather?* I wondered. *What if he dies of a heart attack when the adoption is half-finished?*

More months passed. More pictures arrived. By now both babies were even more adorable. We could hardly wait to get our hands on them. According to the doctor's updates they enjoyed music, were very friendly, smiled, cooed, grasped objects, and did all the things babies that age do. Kaitlyn learned to sit before Kaleb. It must be, we decided, because

45

Kaleb's little legs were too short to compensate for his prodigious tummy.

We enjoyed printing out pictures to show our friends. They rejoiced with us and loved the babies too. Aunt Julia gave us a beautiful pink dress she found at a yard sale. Often when we shopped, Francie and I haunted the baby section of the store, fingering cute little suits and admiring tiny baby shoes. "Can't we buy just one thing?" Francie begged.

"No," I replied. "If the adoption doesn't work out, it will be too hard to have a lot of cute little clothes lying around."

The last time I had talked to Carl, he said the *tutela* should be finished in about a month. That sounded like progress. "We probably have about again as long to wait as we have already waited," I told Francie. "The countdown isn't usually as hard."

After a month had gone by, I called Carl again. "I'm going to talk to the lawyer this afternoon," Carl said. "I'll get back with you." That day passed and the next. No news. The weekend came and went. Still no news. I began to grow uneasy. Twice I called and reached an answering machine. My calls were not returned.

Tuesday afternoon I lay down beside four-year-old Micah to read his nap story. As usual, I promptly fell asleep while he bounced around, flipping from one side to the other. Suddenly, I awoke. A feeling of great dread spread over me. *Something is wrong with this adoption*, I thought. Sleep eluded me, so I shuffled out to the kitchen. My head ached. I placed a basket of clothes on a chair and listlessly folded them.

The next morning as soon as I returned from hauling schoolchildren, I called Carl again.

"I have bad news," he said. "Really bad news."

It turned out the twins' grandfather had demanded a large sum of money for the babies, and had even threatened the lawyer's life. When Social Services became aware of this, they stopped the *tutela* and whisked the babies from foster care to an undisclosed orphanage. This was bad news indeed, because it is very difficult and time-consuming to retrieve babies from the system once they are entrenched.

"What are the orphanages like?" I wondered.

"That's a question you don't want to ask," Carl replied. "Some are good, a few are excellent, and most of them are terrible. But at least they are past the six-months' stage. They have had stimulation and love, and it will stand them in good stead even if they are neglected now."

I called Phil on his cell phone. "Oh, no!" he said. "To think the babies have to suffer because of someone's selfish agenda." We tried to comfort each other with the assurance that God is still in control, but we couldn't help wondering what the babies were experiencing right then. Instead of shining faces and crisp clean clothes, were they now lying in a filthy crib with soiled diapers? Were they crying because there wasn't enough formula? Surely they were bewildered by the sudden turn of events. They seemed so defenseless. But we knew God is not limited in resources like we are.

After our conversation I went upstairs to gather the dirty laundry. Great sobs shook my body and tears ran down like rain. "Lord, I just don't understand," I cried. "I know you love the babies more than we do, but why did they have to be sacrificed on the altar of another's greed? And, O Lord, we did want them so much."

We waited until evening to tell the children. As they went about their normal activities I looked after them sorrowfully. I wished they wouldn't need to know. Is that how God felt about us? After we finished eating supper, Francie wanted to go take a bath. I told her to wait and Phil and I exchanged looks.

"What was that look about?" Conrad asked.

"Mom has something to tell you," Phil replied.

A hush settled momentarily over the family while each one digested the news, then a volley of questions split the silence. Why? Isn't there anything we can do? It is so hard to accept the death of a dream.

That night when I tucked the children into bed, instead of praying, "Help us get Kaleb and Kaitlyn soon, if it's Your will," we prayed, "please take care of Kaleb and Kaitlyn wherever they are."

Chad, who was six, said, "I wish I could make that grandfather go to jail for a hundred years without anything to eat."

"Well, Chad," I remonstrated, "we need to let God take care of the grandfather."

"It makes me kinda sad," Micah squeaked, and he violently rubbed his eyes with his fists.

A dull ache sat in the bottom of our hearts. Why?

We have always believed that God, in His goodness, allows things to come into our lives to bring us out at the right place. And we still believe that. If we could have seen the whole picture the way God does, we would have marveled at His perfect plan. And so by faith we knew that God was still good, even when we didn't understand.

Our adoption coordinator, Carl Hocke, said they would give us the next referral. I didn't care. My heart felt like wood. I was afraid to hope again. We knew we really wanted another child, but who could take the place in our hearts of Kaleb and Kaitlyn?

As time went by, I began to wonder if God had introduced the idea of twins because He really wanted us to take more than one, and that's the only way we would have considered it. Maybe there were two children out there designed for us. I suggested the idea to Phil, and he said he'd thought of the same thing. I talked to Carl and he said it could be arranged.

Almost three months rolled by before the new referrals

came. Little Brian Alexander was about a month old, and
Dairyn Michelle was a little over one week. We changed
their names to Donovan Jose and Merideth Fern.

Because the babies weren't twins, we were going to have
to come up with another dossier before the case could go to
court. I could hardly gather the strength to make up the new
dossier. Although I should have been delighted, I felt dis-
heartened and tired. I would've been happy with the new
babies but I told myself they probably wouldn't work out
either. I felt the whole thing was destined to failure from its
bad beginning. When baby pictures started arriving via e-
mail I didn't dare let myself become attached.

In spite of all my negative thinking, Carl told us to be
ready to fly the last week in May. Donovan's paperwork was
complete, but the other lawyer didn't seem overly motivated,
and it could take as long as three months until Merideth's
paperwork would be ready. We could either let Donovan
stay in foster care longer, or we could plan to make two trips.
We didn't want to leave Donovan in foster care one minute
longer than necessary. We would make two trips.

How exciting to pack our bags for another baby! I gathered enough little boy things to last for a week, along with
all the fun things like baby powder, bottles, and squeezable
toys.

Carl Hocke had previously reserved a room for us at the
Radisson Hotel in Guatemala City. He told us someone
would be waiting for us, carrying a sign bearing our names.
When we arrived in Guatemala, we puzzled our way out to
the front of the airport and sure enough, in a few minutes
we spotted a dapper young man, wearing a red vest and
white shirt holding our names aloft on a cardboard sign. He
asked how our trip was and if this is the first time to
Guatemala and helped us tote our luggage to the curb. He
said he had three more people to pick up and wondered if

we would mind waiting.

After our group had assembled, he hustled off into the darkness and soon returned with a white Mitsubishi van. We loaded up and joined the honking, jostling vehicles racing at high speed through the streets.

Ten minutes later he stopped in front of an elegant, many-storied hotel. A large glass front with revolving glass doors and a doorman, graced the top of the wide stone veranda. Inside the tiled lobby, three receptionists waited on clients behind a curved mahogany desk. Four clocks showing the time in Guatemala, New York, Tokyo, and Inglaterra adorned a mahogany paneled wall behind the counter. To the left was a restaurant with white cloth napkins folded in pyramids on china plates. On the right a spiral staircase wound toward a second-story bar. Straight ahead a fountain of water cascaded over rocks. Lush green plants adorned the edges of the waterfall and a wide staircase ascended behind it.

The receptionist, who handed us a key for our room, gave us a little folder with six free breakfast coupons and two coupons for the bar tucked inside. The elevator, built of mahogany and mirrors, glided to the eleventh floor. We soon located our room by the gold-colored numbers over the door. Because the hallway leading to our room was rather narrow, I was unprepared for the spacious apartment which opened to our view.

Several lamps shed a soft glow over a living area with a couch and two armchairs. A twelve-foot-wide window covered by sheers and both light- and heavy-weight drapes stretched from floor to ceiling. A kitchenette with a microwave occupied one corner. A king-sized bed monopolized the bedroom and another twelve-foot window looked out on the street far below.

Sunlight streaming in our window at 6:30 and workmen

hammering away on a hotel under construction just down the street roused us Tuesday morning. Since we didn't need to meet with our lawyer, Zulma, until nine or ten o'clock, Phil decided to explore our little part of the city.

Left alone in the motel room, I began to wonder what in the world we were doing adopting another baby. *Phil is almost fifty years old,* I told myself. *He could be thinking about grandchildren, maybe, but not another baby of his own to raise.* Even though Phil had agreed to this adoption, I knew he never would have been the aggressor in it and the weight of responsibility sagged on my shoulders. I thought about all the money it takes to raise a child and Phil could look forward to tapering off the workforce before too many years if we stopped adopting children. Money is really the lesser stress, though, when a person considers all the training and watching for souls and guiding and giving direction for years and years and years. *We're into it too far to back out now,* I decided. *We'll just have to trust the Lord to work it out if we made a bad move. If we can raise him for the Lord, we couldn't do anything more worthwhile, but who knows if he'll turn out for the Lord?*

I studied my Sunday school lesson so that I'd be prepared to teach on Sunday without staying up all Saturday night getting ready.

Around 10:00 the phone rang. It was Zulma. "We'll be there in a few minutes," she said. I went back to my studying, but I had to press my pen hard on the paper to keep my hands from shaking as I wrote my notes. I hoped Phil would hurry back, so that he could get those first-moment pictures. Sure enough, soon after he returned, the phone rang again and the receptionist said, "There is someone in the lobby who would like to see you."

I quickly brushed my teeth and slipped on my shoes and with thumping heart followed Phil to the elevator.

51

When we entered the lobby, the first thing I saw was a tall, dark-haired woman wearing a red and black dress. The top left quarter and the bottom right quarter were black and the corresponding quarters were red. She held a large packet of papers under her arm. Beside her stood a small woman wearing a flimsy summer dress, holding a darling baby boy with his thumb in his mouth. We shook hands and Zulma asked if we would like to go up to our room. On the upward ride I caressed the baby with my eyes, from the top of his even-length black hair on his flat little head to his little brown shoes. One eyelid drooped ever so charmingly over almost oriental eyes. He had a tiny little nose with the ittiest, bittiest noseholes and a wide eager smile as I chucked him under his chin. I'm sure we talked on the way up, but I don't remember anything about it.

When we arrived in our suite, Zulma asked if I would like to hold the baby, and I happily assented. He smiled and reached his hands toward my face. He didn't seem at all shy, but he didn't cuddle either. He pressed his little arms against my chest and rared back to look at my face. He seemed to like to sputter, and when he splattered my nose and I reacted, he grinned. Phil kept snapping pictures, and I sat down with Zulma and the foster mother to talk over the baby's schedule and habits. The foster mother spoke only Spanish so Zulma interpreted. She gave me a typed food and nap schedule, and said he has been very healthy. She said when he wants attention he coughs. In a yellow bag she brought a bottle already prepared for his next feeding, one can of formula, another of cereal, juice, baby food, and a few Pampers.

Zulma went over the papers with me for the next day's interview with the consulate. "Tomorrow morning you need to meet me in the lobby at quarter to seven to go to the embassy," she said.

"Quarter to seven?" we asked.

"Yes. There will be maybe ten couples to go for an interview and we need to get there early."

After they left we played with Donovan. I wanted to see him roll over like his foster mother said, so I laid him on the floor and dangled a stuffed Pooh bear to one side. I noticed he reached for the toy but when his hand touched it, he did not close his fingers. I held the bear closer and again he merely batted at it. I took his hand and closed it over Pooh, but he only held it briefly.

Tossing the toy aside, I tried to get him to close his hand over my fingers. He could do it, but his grip was not very strong. When I tried to raise him to a standing position, he quickly let go. I tried to stand him on his feet but his legs folded up under him much as Francie's had when she was a baby. A sick little feeling started inside. *What if he's not normal?* I wondered. Suddenly raising a healthy infant didn't seem like a major task at all compared to what we could be facing. When I tried to set him on the couch, he slumped forward or rared back. I could see he was nowhere close to sitting alone. Through this extensive examination, Donovan cooed and spit and laughed.

I remembered worrying about Francie. I had even taken her to the doctor who assured me she just wasn't aware of her feet down there; one of these times she'd wake up. I watched the progress of babies near her age and grew clear sick with worry. It happened like the doctor said it would. She's fine now, and I often told myself afterward I would not waste precious time worrying if I ever had another baby like that. I reminded myself of all that, sitting in the motel room. *Besides,* I thought, *if he's not normal he needs us to care for him more than ever.* Phil said he thought we'd see a big difference in another month. "He may not have had much stimulation in foster care." Donovan had such a passive personality. He lay on the floor and cooed to himself and when we walked past he'd grin so personably. "That's probably another reason his motor skills aren't developed," we told each other.

On one of his walks, Phil had discovered a little "hole in the wall" restaurant not far from the hotel. The place had room for only six or eight small tables and we sat on little folding stools. It was split level and we ate on the upper level next to the kitchen where it was very warm. For four dollars we got plates of fried chicken, rice, tortillas, and soup.

Donovan slept from 9:30 p.m. to 4:30 in the morning. I fed him a bottle, and he played for awhile. When he finally settled, it was almost time to get around for our morning appointment. Phil went for breakfast and met another couple from NC who were adopting a baby boy and also had an appointment at the embassy.

Zulma came to pick us up in her little Nissan soon after six-thirty. We zigzagged in and out of traffic, took a little back street, and jerked to a halt on a little concrete pad beside a dingy building. It didn't look like the embassy to me, but I didn't know where else we'd be going. Zulma motioned us through the open doorway where a secretary sat at a desk. In a matter of a few minutes about ten more American-looking couples with dark babies swarmed inside. Zulma swooped Donovan out of my arms. Before I knew what was happening, she had disappeared around a corner. I ducked my head around to see where she was taking my baby, then I realized they were taking pictures for his visa.

From here we went across the street to the US Embassy, where we waited our turn for a security check. Once inside the building we understood the need to get there early. There were at least 50 people sitting on chairs and leaning against the walls, waiting their turns to speak to an agent. Zulma took our fat envelope full of precious documents and stood in line. After about 30 minutes she gave our envelopes to the person behind the window, and informed us we would be called when it was time for our interview. The interview itself lasted only about ten or fifteen minutes, and we were told to come back in the afternoon to pick up the visa.

Until the moment an adoptive parent has the visa in hand, there is always the chance something will go awry. I breathed a sigh of relief when Phil returned that afternoon with a large, sealed manila envelope. We were set to go!

As we flew out of Guatemala the next day with our precious little Donovan, we could hardly wait to show him to the rest of the family. There was so much love in store for him!

Donovan responded immediately to the stimulation he received from all his big brothers and Francie. He developed so fast we felt like he turned into a little boy before we were quite ready to release the baby part of him.

Merideth's lawyer, Andres, wrapped up her adoption faster than we thought he would, and almost exactly a month after we traveled for Donovan, we flew into Guatemala City for the second time. Andres said he would meet with us and the foster parents at four o'clock in the hotel lobby. I kept an eye on the street below from our bedroom window. Whenever a car stopped in the vicinity of the hotel, I watched the doors pop open and counted how many people climbed out. I thought I'd be sure to spot the baby's arrival but while I was still looking, Phil entered the room.

"They're here!" he announced. And there stood Andres. It took only one glance to see a short man with a brightly striped shirt, a lady with a silver-lined tooth, and a girl about nine years old with fluffy brown hair. Then my eyes fastened on a round-faced baby with a head full of shiny black hair. Our little daughter at last!

Merideth came to me without hesitation. Her large dark eyes studied my face intently. I stroked her beautiful hair and wondered what her personality was like. The foster father could speak some English, and he told me in great detail about her schedule. Obviously, Merideth had received a lot of loving attention in their home. "She likes music and dancing," he said. "Watch this." And he said something to his daughter in Spanish. She began to sway and sing a jazzy little tune. Merideth immediately began swaying too. The foster mother gave me a little album of snapshots of Merideth's babyhood up to this point, as well as a little lock of her hair and a plastic case with her shriveled umbilical cord.

The father took her and held her up. "You like the baby?" he asked. "You like her face?"

"I like her very much," I replied.

All this while Phil and Andres were going over the documents and plans for meeting at the embassy in the morning.

And then it was time for them to go. Merideth's foster family kissed her with tears in their eyes and walked out of the room. Phil went to the store, and I was left alone to play with our new little baby. She had a yellow jumper on over top a lot of bumpy underclothes and I thought she seemed rather warm. I took off three layers of clothes down to her diaper and T-shirt. And then she suddenly seemed to realize she was alone in a strange place with a strange woman. She started to cry as hard as she could, and although I tried to comfort her I could not give her the thing she needed most in the world—a familiar pair of arms. She refused the bottle and refused to be distracted by toys. I walked the floor with her until she fell asleep.

When she awoke, she seemed happy and contented. About the middle of the night, she had another crying spell and refused to be comforted. I felt so sorry for her, but I could only whisper into her hair that everything would be all right.

It took Merideth a little longer to limber up at home than it had taken Donovan, but after a few days she had taken residence in everyone's heart. Francie especially loved her and took over the task of bathing her and combing her hair. At long last her prayers for a sister had been answered!

Curious people have often asked us, "Don't you have any children of your own?"

I know they don't mean any harm, so I squelch the urge to say, "Yes, eight of 'em," and reply, "We don't have any biological children."

Chad is the only one of our children whose biological mother we have had contact with. She came to our home several times when Chad was younger, but she doesn't want him to know she is his mother.

Phil, Conrad, and Harlan all work with Pantego Overhead Garage Door Company. It is a family-owned business, and we are thankful for the opportunity to be a part of it. Deryk works at the warehouse evenings after school.

We are members of Hope Mennonite Church which is part of the Nationwide Fellowship. Our three oldest boys have made commitments to the Lord, for which we are very thankful. Our children are well accepted in the church and school, and we appreciate the openness in our brotherhood toward adoption. After all, adopted children are like everyone else; they have normal childhood spats and normal teenage growing pains. While it is true they may have a certain sense of rejection to deal with, especially if they are older when they become part of the family, it seems important to us not to make concessions or become defensive of them. Rather, present them with choices and encourage them to move forward.

We enjoy the challenge of our children, although

sometimes we feel like it stretches our resources to instruct and encourage the older ones, train the in-between ones, and still find enough energy to keep up with the little ones.

God has been very good to us, and in choosing this path for us to acquire our family, He chose well.

Hannah's Baby Boy

(May be sung to the tune of
"Here We Go Round the Mulberry Bush.")

*Hannah wanted a baby boy,
A baby boy, a baby boy;
Hannah wanted a baby boy
To hold in her arms and love.*

*She prayed to God to send her a child,
To send her a child, to send her a child;
She prayed to God to send her a child;
And God heard her prayer from above.*

*God sent a baby to answer her prayer,
To answer her prayer, to answer her prayer;
God sent a baby to answer her prayer;
And she loved her baby boy.*

*Hannah took Samuel back to the Lord,
Back to the Lord, back to the Lord;
Hannah took Samuel back to the Lord
With her heart full of grateful joy.*

—Edith E. Cutting

5

Thomas & Rhoda Bontrager

Anthony — *January 23, 1990*
Jennifer — *May 18, 1993*
Jaran — *May 23, 1995*
Lorinda — *September 12, 1998*

—Goshen, Indiana

After the crushing blow of having our doctor announce, "You have no chance of ever having children," a kind medical assistant gently opened to us the door of adoption. As an adult adoptee, she had a very positive experience to share. We never struggled with the idea of adopting–it was something we both felt we wanted to do. As a former teacher, I had two students who had been adopted into loving families. We prayed and sought God's will and came away feeling privileged that God did have a plan for us, and in His time, He would bless our home through adoption. After we felt led to adopt, we spent many hours researching and making phone calls. We contacted churches, doctors, attorneys, high schools, colleges, and any other leads we were given. Lutheran Social Services put us on their list.

In the meantime, after our first crushing disappointment, a teacher friend told us about a private maternity home through which relatives of hers had adopted twins. We contacted the home, and after doing the necessary paperwork, were put on their list too.

Eventually, we were chosen by a young girl who had been

urged to have an abortion, but courageously chose to give life. She said, "What I did was wrong, but I know God can make good come out of it." After four months of going to the doctor with her, making visits and phone calls, she presented us with the gift of our first son! We had thought seeing his ultrasound was exciting, but that was nothing compared to the feeling that coursed through us when she placed him in my arms. We were thrilled and knew God had kept Anthony for us. It was hard to believe it finally had happened. Finally, it was our baby crying for us; we had bottles to fill, little clothes to buy and wash, and someone to rock and cuddle. Anthony was born on his Grandpa Bontrager's birthday, which we thought was special.

Thomas Bontrager family

After he was ten months old, we again paid our retaining fees to the maternity home and worked our way through the legalities of the foreign adoptions they were pursuing at that time. After being cleared with immigration and with passports in hand ready to fly to Mexico at a moment's notice to pick up our second baby, we discovered this lady had left the country and was having a high time with over $170,000.00 from forty or more couples. Our efforts, money, and worst of all, our dreams, were down the drain. We tried to pick up the pieces and again turned to Lutheran Social Services, but also made other contacts.

In time, we met a young birthmother through Lutheran, but we had not been told whether she chose us or not. Then suddenly, we got a call from them telling us we had a daughter. After all we had been through in the last three-and-a-half years, we could scarcely believe this little black-haired girl was truly ours. Several years later we got a letter through the agency from a relative of the birthmother. She told us how she had been thinking she was getting this baby, and when she went to the hospital to pick her up, they told her the family the birthmother had chosen had already picked her up. She was very upset! But now she was writing to tell us that after she had seen the progress letters and pictures we had sent the birthmother, she sincerely felt the Lord wanted Jennifer in our home instead of with an old lady like her. Now she was rejoicing with us! After that letter, we appreciated even more the miracle of Jennifer joining our family! This relative has since written us beautiful letters.

Baby number three was another son! My mother had given us their old phone book so that we could turn it in at McDonald's for a hamburger, but we forgot to do so. In it I found the phone number for a networking agency on the West Coast, and the results were worth more than any hamburger! We had worked with ten birthmothers in six months' time with all of them choosing "at the last minute," to do the parenting themselves. Sometimes birthmothers may lead several couples along at the same time, stirring their hopes to be able to adopt.

When I talked to Jaran's birthmother, we discovered we had many similar likes and dislikes—he was due on our anniversary, and she thought if the baby was a boy she would've named him Anthony, although she knew we would name him. She was very pleased when I told her we already had an Anthony. We had planned with the birth-mother for this birth in Indiana because she wanted me to be with her at the time of birth. I guess our baby thought otherwise! He was born early and put in his appearance in California. So we flew to California and he became ours at one day old. We spent an enjoyable week with the birth-mother, her mother, and grandmother while interstate legal-ities were taken care of.

It was difficult for us to leave, knowing her pain was our gain. She thanked us many times for giving him a chance in life. In spite of her love she couldn't think of raising a child singly in the drug- and gang-infested area in which she lived. Working through the Silver Spoon agency was a real roller-coaster ride, but God again in His own time gave us the child He had chosen for us.

We had wanted very much to add one more to our fam-ily, but knew the odds were stacked against us—our age, the fact that we already had three children, plus adoption and medical expenses had really drained us financially. Most agencies would no longer work with us because of those fac-tors. We committed it to the Lord and also told our worker at Lutheran Social Services about our desires. Our children prayed earnestly for a tiny baby sister. They had a new cousin four days old, and they wanted to know if their uncle and aunt had prayed more than we did!

I was putting them to bed rather late on a Saturday evening, and again they prayed for a tiny baby. As we got up from our knees the phone rang. It was our social worker! What could she want on a Saturday night? I thought maybe she was telling me about a temporary foster home needed for a baby that she had mentioned to me earlier, because three days earlier she had told me there were no prospective adoptions coming up for the agency. But no, she was telling me she had a baby for us for keeps!

The birthmother had told no one she was pregnant until the baby was born at home. She was then taken to the hospital and the hospital chose to call our social worker. Our social worker first called a couple who had been on the waiting list for eight years. They had one child and decided their lives were perfect, so they were no longer interested. Next, she tried calling two couples who had no children but neither one answered the phone. Finally, she got the feeling we were praying and felt led to call us! The birthmother had only asked that she choose a Christian home. Of course we wanted her!

Lorinda entered the world quickly, made a speedy entrance into our family, and has gone at high speed ever since! Everything happened so fast, and we had so much fun calling people with this unexpected news! Our children's faith in prayer was certainly strengthened, and now they had a sister only four days younger than her cousin! The birthmother's family chose to help with expenses, which made it a double miracle.

Yes, God truly cared about our family and, through all the experiences we had, we can say, *"Hitherto hath the Lord helped us."* We deeply appreciate the caring support of our adoption group, family, friends, our church family, and the teachers at Harrison Christian School.

God miraculously filled our hearts and home and like

Hannah of old, we, too, praise Him for His goodness and dedicate our little ones to God and His work.

Our encouragement to others—Don't give up when it gets rough, the right ones do work out for you. We worked with 25 birthmothers and have four children!

We live on a dairy farm near Goshen, Indiana. We are members of the Yellow Creek Wisler Mennonite Church.

6

John & Cindy Culp

Crystal Rebecca — *February 13, 1989*

Shobhana Joy — *July 2, 1992*

—Halsey, Oregon

On February 13, 1989, my mother and I were waiting in a small lobby in the obstetrics section of the Goshen hospital in northern Indiana. I was about forty-two-and-a-half at the time. My pregnant wife Cindy (a few weeks my elder) had been taken into the operating room nearby. The baby in her womb was in a "breech" position, and Cindy's doctor had advised a surgical "C-section" delivery. He had said the delivery would last only a few minutes.

"Mr. Culp." I looked at a pediatrician whose name I had heard, but whom I had not met. *What did he want?* Then I saw that he was holding a plump little girl, whose damp bluish-black hair lay in curls against her head. As I gingerly took our baby Crystal from his arms, I remembered the wonder I had felt over ten years before when I held my first nephew, the firstborn of my sister Ruth and her husband, Sam Kropf. I also remembered what an atheistic, evolution-believing instructor had told my father after the birth of the instructor's first child. "There is something about the birth of a child that almost makes you a believer."

In the summer of 1995, we moved to Oregon. There were a lot of practical adjustments to make—new home, new work, new places for auto repair, new places to shop, etc. Before long, however, we were thinking again of adoption.

We were now living in a larger house, though rented (we owned the one in Indiana), and my income was now higher. Crystal was now six years old, and all three of us felt adoption might be good.

Years before, I had met some people associated with Holt International Children's Services, an adoption agency in Eugene, Oregon. Ruth had introduced us to some programs of PLAN, "Plan Loving Adoption Now, Inc.," an agency in

John Culp family

McMinnville, Oregon. David and Sheryl Kunkel had already used the services of PLAN. Only one child was born to them—Keith, a boy with Down's syndrome. Through a PLAN program they adopted a girl, Diana (deeAHnah), from Colombia. They were thinking about adopting another child. They also gave us information on PLAN international adoption programs.

On Monday evening (February 5), we were able to drive to Eugene for the first pre-adopt session at Holt, which we found very interesting. The next Monday evening we took a second session at Holt. This was also informative—and sobering. One staff worker inquired about my income to see if it was legally sufficient for us to have a two-child family through adoption. We were quite impressed with Holt, but their international programs required that the parents be not over forty years older than the child being adopted. They also stressed that the child adopted should not be older than the oldest (or only) child in the adoptive family. Cindy and I were both 42½ years older than Crystal. A staff worker said that we could request an exception, but we decided to look at other options first.

On February 21 David and Sheryl invited us to go along to see a video at PLAN about a new Siberia program. The video showed both babies and children in several orphanages. At one place a group of children of preschool age were outside in the snow, dressed warmly in coats and hoods. For one moment a little girl with brown hair and brown eyes came into focus, and then the camera moved on, but Cindy had seen the girl she wanted. Sheryl picked out a blond, blue-eyed girl almost six, and David picked out a couple of interest to him, including a black-haired, dark-eyed, brown-skinned girl.

The Kunkels were ready to move ahead and pick a child, but we had not committed ourselves to any program yet.

69

While Cindy had found the girl she wanted, I was not so sure.

In May we attended a banquet hosted by PLAN at which Don Hawkinson spoke. He told of some interesting and moving experiences in Russia, and he concluded with some Bible principles concerning children. On August 30 we went to a PLAN meeting to hear Dr. Alex. We had seen him on the videos, and now we were hearing him in person. A woman had come with him, and we were told she was a Russian lawyer. We enjoyed hearing Dr. Alex and were able to meet him afterward. Cindy and Sheryl had taken the first video to a place in Corvallis, and they obtained a black and white print of the little girl Cindy wanted. She gave this to Alex, and he said he would try to find out if the girl was available. On the day they left, we went to the Portland airport with David and Sheryl to bid them farewell.

At the PLAN meeting where we heard Dr. Alex, a staff worker had told us about a new India program, through PLAN. The other India program only offered babies, but this one had children. It sounded interesting to me, but by this time we had both decided to pursue trying to get the girl from Siberia, if she was available. In September I finished my autobiography—Cindy had hers done before—and we had all the required paperwork handed in. In October we had our home study. We were now ready to request a child through the Siberia program.

This Siberia program required that the parents go to Russia to complete things there and pick up the child. I wanted very much to figure out a way that a trip to eastern Russia could include visits in Thailand and Malaysia, but I never figured out how to do that.

In February of 1997 we were sent a picture of the little girl whom IFI (International Families Inc.) had picked out for us. When Judy, our PLAN representative, received the picture, she did not agree with Mr. Rao. She told me that she told him, 'That little girl is not a Culp.' (It reminded me of people who choose their newborn's name after they have seen it so that its name will fit.) Because Judy felt so strongly about it, she sent two other pictures with it. One was that of Shobhana, a girl from India. I didn't recognize her as our daughter at first, but I just kept coming back to that picture all day, and by the time Crystal came home from school, I had already bonded to our daughter Shobhana.

I can hardly think of rejecting one needy little girl in favor of another, but a choice needed to be made, and in this case we were cleared to adopt only one. We had prayed that the Lord would lead us to the child He had for us, and that is the precious part of this story. The little girl that IFI picked out for us seemed to be a healthy little girl. The one that the Lord had for us had apparently had polio as a baby, and she walked with a limp. But that did not matter, because I sensed that Shobhana was the answer to our prayers. And so now it is no surprise to me when people tell me that Shobhana looks like our family. On March 3, 1997, I called Judy to tell her we wanted Shobhana.

Before we had changed to the India program, I had asked if we could go get the girl, rather than having her escorted by someone else to this country, as was usually the case, and I had been told there was no reason we couldn't.

On February 12, David and Sheryl Kunkel flew to Moscow to eventually bring back Alevtina, the light-haired and blue-eyed girl on the video with the big smile. From Moscow they would fly to Irkutsk. On March 7 they flew into the Portland airport with Alevtina. There they were met by a group of us that included Sheryl's mother, a friend with her daughter, the two Kunkel children, the three in our family, my sister Helen (who knew some Russian), and two staff workers from PLAN. The ones from PLAN had a second picture of Shobhana, similar to the first, but a little closer up.

The records on Shobhana indicated that she had come to the orphanage on July 2, 1996. Her birth date was given as July 2, 1992. Around April of 1997 we were sent another picture of her. The lighting was different, and it hardly looked like the same girl, but the way she stood was similar. Several months later another photograph came, and this looked much like the previous one, except that it was taken closer up and there was a trace of a smile. Later a video would come showing various children, including Shobhana wearing a dress that Cindy had made and sent to her. We had tried to calculate her size from her records and her pictures, but the dress was a size 6 and she was about size 4. In the video, we could see Shobhana walk around, respond to her name, talk a little to others, but we never saw a hint of a smile.

Fall came and then winter. I studied how to plan my itinerary. Cindy had decided that she did not want to travel along after all.

It may have been in March of 1998 that our caseworker at PLAN asked Cindy if I was still planning on traveling to India, and she seemed a little surprised when Cindy told her I was. A month or so later we were told it was not going to work for me to travel to India to get Shobhana. On top of that, we were told that the escort fee was now $3000.00 instead of the $2500.00 charge we had been given a year before. On top of that, we learned that being escorted to this country meant that she would be coming—not to Portland, the international airport two hours away, or Seattle, a few hours further north—but to Washington, D.C., almost at the opposite end of the country. I asked PLAN for some explanations.

First, I asked why I was told that I could not go for

Shobhana after being told a year before that I could. Secondly, I wanted to know why the escort fee was increased. And thirdly, I asked if there was any information on Shobhana's background. The director of IFI (International Families, Inc.—he and his family immigrated from India) sent a reply to our caseworker at PLAN, and she faxed it to me. The reasons given for why I couldn't go were these: a family had traveled to India and stayed as guests at the orphanage, but they took advantage of their privileges and brought back a bad report. Also, they said that since my wife was not going, there were concerns about how Shobhana would feel about going with a strange man. The IFI director also listed expenses involved in escorting Shobhana that added up to over $4000.00.

We had been told it was important that we not try to find out who the mother was. The IFI director did give a very brief account of Shobhana's background, which we were told was confidential. What we were told did sound to me like something that could happen in India, but I was rather skeptical by this time.

I saw no point in arguing about their reasons for why I should not go. I was sure God could have worked it out for me to go if He had felt that I needed to at this time. I was relieved in a sense not to have to spend time in Bombay with a little girl, but I was also keenly disappointed not to be going.

Finally on March 30, we were pleased to hear from PLAN that Shobhana's paperwork in India had been approved and we were officially her legal guardians. On April 20, Judy Elkins returned from a trip to Washington, D.C., with our guardianship papers.

The final step was to file the I-600 with the Immigration and Naturalization Service (INS). I flubbed up this time and sent these to the wrong address, so it was May 13 until our paperwork made it to an examiner's desk. A week later we received a letter from INS asking for an addendum to our home study. PLAN helped us—they sent more papers for us to sign and return to them. Judy then sent these to INS and they acknowledged receipt on May 28.

About this time we received a call from Amish friends in northern Indiana that they were coming west for a visit to Oregon and California. Would we be able to take them to see the Oregon coast? They called on June 17 to confirm that they were to arrive by train on July 27th. We thought it was safe to arrange to take them because we had faith that Shobhana would be arriving by the end of June.

Then it dawned on me that way back there in December of 1996, when we were cleared by INS to adopt a foreign child, we were told that this approval would be good for 18 months. If we didn't have our child by the end of 18 months, we would have to start all over with INS. When I thought of how long (eight months to be exact) it had taken to be approved by INS in 1996, I began to get panicky. I did not want to wait another eight months to get Shobhana home. So I started searching for advice and praying for guidance. Somewhere along the line I was told of someone in another adoption quandary who had asked his senator for help.

Consequently, I called Senator Gordon Smith and told his secretary of our plight. This secretary was hired solely to deal with INS cases, and she knew just what to advise me to do. I was to write up our case and fax it to the senator. I stated that I realized that we were "just another set of paper-work," but that I felt it would be good if INS could "have a heart" for this child. This being June 4th, I was wondering how we could possibly have our child by June 12 (when our 18 months expired) if something didn't happen fast. Thus I authorized the senator to receive information and make inquiries about this matter in our behalf.

I was almost as miserable as a nine-months-pregnant mother who is past her due date! What if we couldn't get our paperwork cleared by INS on time and had to start all over again with the I-600A? And then on June 16th, INS approved our I-600 application and sent Form 171 (Notice of Approval of Relative Immigrant Visa Petition). They also told us that a cable had been sent to New Delhi on that date clearing Shobhana to travel. It hadn't seemed to matter that it was past the 18-month expiration date. Or did it? Had Senator Smith interceded for us somehow?

In June we were told that Shobhana could be coming in July. An awful thought came to me. I called our caseworker at PLAN and told her to make sure that Shobhana did not come on July 27 or even a day or two before or after. Our Amish friends were coming by train to Portland on July 27, after spending time in Montana where they had once lived. Our caseworker said she could not guarantee that Shobhana would not come on that day, but she would do what she could.

As the time drew near to go East to pick up Shobhana, David and Sheryl proved to be a real help to us. David was able to get a couple good deals on airline tickets. Sheryl agreed to go with Cindy. In addition to accompanying Cindy, Sheryl would be bringing a baby from India to Oregon for a couple who were getting this infant.

Sheryl Kunkel and Cindy flew to D.C. on Saturday, July 27. Things went well for them, and about noon they were in Dulles airport and found where international flights come in. Since they had a little time before Shobhana's supposed arrival, they went for a bite of lunch and were soon back waiting. When 2:30 came and went and they saw no signs of Shobhana, they started inquiring. They were told that if she was on a United flight, she would arrive at a different concourse, so they took the shuttle over to that concourse, which was close to where they were to fly out at 5:40 p.m., but the place was all but deserted. They were told they had no record of her there, so they went back to the first place and waited and inquired some more. They seemed to be getting nowhere. Finally they reasoned they had better split up, and one of them stay at each place. Sheryl stayed in the United concourse, and Cindy headed back to the main international gate. Cindy was told by the baggage police that we could talk to Immigration at 5:00 if Shobhana was not there by that time.

In the meantime, Sheryl got on the phone to her husband at home in Oregon, and he called Judy at PLAN. He told her about their problems and asked her to call the airport and see if Shobhana was there and try to speed things up for them. About 4:50 Shobhana appeared through the doors with Mrs. Rao, who was pushing Neha in a stroller. With our dear friend at the other concourse, there was no one to take pictures of Cindy meeting Shobhana. Cindy hugged her, smiled through her tears, and hugged Shobhana some more, before she remembered that she must get her and Neha over to the other concourse. She told the Raos that she needed to leave quickly, so their son and his friend helped her get to the shuttle bus. As they were standing in line, Mr. Rao hurried up and asked to see the two passports he had given Cindy. One of them was the wrong one, so they quickly exchanged and soon boarded the shuttle. After they got off the shuttle, Cindy pushed the stroller with Shobhana in it and perched Neha on her hip, not to mention carrying her backpack and the bags full of the little girls' meager belongings.

Sheryl saw Cindy coming and ran to help. The last person was getting ready to board the flight to Portland. Cindy had both tickets, so she had no choice but to wait, which she would have done anyway. Somehow they managed to find

76

their tickets, board the plane, and collapse into their seats. Neha was not feeling well. She did not eat much and slept most of the time. We found out later that she had the start of pneumonia. Cindy was so glad that Sheryl was along to hold her, for she was nearly exhausted. Shobhana seemed very happy to be with her new mother, and she had fun with the tablet, pencils, coloring book, and crayons Cindy had brought for her. She wasn't very hungry either and slept the last two hours of the flight.

As soon as their plane stopped at the gate where they were to deplane, they quickly got busy changing the little girls' dresses. Consequently, they were the last ones off the plane. Shobhana stole the hearts of those who were waiting by having big smiles for everyone. We have pictures to show this because David, Sheryl's husband, there with the three children, was on the ball with his camera. John's family—his parents, his sister Helen, and his sister Ruth with her husband Jason and their large family—had all come together in Jason's large van, and they had brought Crystal to meet her new sister.

Neha's new parents were also on hand to get their child. It was quite a good-sized group that gathered to welcome the arrival of the new girl for our family. But where was the new daddy? He was out at a park south of Newport along the coast, where he had taken our Amish friends in a van he had borrowed. Was I ever disappointed that I could not be present at the grand arrival! Having worked through my disappointment in not being able to travel to get her, this seemed almost minor in comparison. Yes, I was not the first man in Oregon to pick up the new girl in his arms, but I was the one who was to have the privilege of being her father.

The girl from India, who had seemed so sober in the pictures, smiled easily. I was surprised how small she seemed. I had tried to calculate her size from the information we had been given about her, but she was smaller than we expected. It was a couple days before I felt she was ready for me to pick her up, but it was not long before she was willing to walk with me outside.

We had been told that Shobhana had a "slight limp." At times the limp was barely noticeable, but it became very pronounced if she tried to run, and she seemed to fall easily, especially if she got off balance a little. Her left leg was noticeably thinner than the right one, and we noticed that she sometimes used her right leg to help lift her left leg when she got into the car. A specialist pointed out to us that when Shobhana was seated with her legs hanging, she could not move her left foot forward, due to lack of certain muscles in her leg. He recommended that we take her for an evaluation at the Shriners hospital in Portland.

She was thought to be six years old when she came. She could not ride a bicycle. Crystal could ride a bicycle before she was six. Even riding a tricycle was difficult for Shobhana except on a downhill grade. She could walk, however, and it helped to have someone hold her left hand.

A couple years later, we went to the coast with the Kunkels for the day. We followed a trail back to an overlook above the Pacific Ocean, where some were watching for whales to come up for air. I wanted Shobhana to walk for a while, and I took her hand to help her on the trail. I told her I would carry her on my back when she got tired. She walked the two-mile trail on her own feet. One of the first times I tried to help her ride a small bicycle, she somehow bounced off and landed on the sidewalk. But she kept trying to learn. It seemed difficult for her to concentrate on both pedaling and balancing the bicycle. Then one day when she was eight, she showed us that she could ride her bicycle by herself. Learning to "roller-blade" has proved difficult, but she has been trying, and in the fourth grade, she learned to "jump rope" with others.

I wanted to learn some Gujarati now that we had a girl who spoke that language, but I never made much progress, and in the meantime Shobhana was learning more English and losing the language she had known. When she first came, it was Crystal who seemed to understand her best, and she sometimes told us what she understood Shobhana to be saying, even though Crystal spoke English, and Shobhana knew little but her language from India.

Shobhana and Crystal both had a lot of adjustments to make. While Shobhana liked ice cream, candy, and things like that, she did not like many of the foods we ate. For a while she ate mostly bananas because there seemed to be so few things she liked. We tried to be kind but firm. We tried to coax her. Sometimes our efforts did not seem successful, but she did not starve.

Crystal had been used to sleeping by herself, but now had to share the bed with a sister, and one who seemed to always end up on Crystal's side of the bed. Crystal had been looking forward to a sister who could do things with her, but there were many things that Shobhana could not do. Things have not always gone smoothly in the family. Adding a girl to the family added another human being, and we learned that Shobhana did not always smile. We sometimes wondered if a time of crisis might come, as it has in some adoptions.

We were rather tired of paperwork by the time Shobhana arrived, and we told PLAN that we preferred to concentrate on learning to know our new daughter and helping her get acquainted with her new surroundings before proceeding with naturalization. We did need to apply for a temporary social security number before we could file our income tax reports for 1998, though. We waited until the end of 1999 before we contacted a lawyer to help us through the naturalization process.

Shobhana received her Oregon birth certificate on February 16, 2000. Again we filed a form (N-643) with INS, but with much less anxiety. We were notified to appear at the INS office in Portland on September 6, 2000, for the naturalization paperwork to be completed. On that day Shobhana Joy Culp became a citizen of the United States of America. The final step with paperwork was to apply for a permanent social security number. Shobhana received that identification number in January of 2001.

We have told a lot of our experiences, but I suppose anyone who reads this will realize there is more that could have been said. Also, the story has not yet ended. It is the desire of both of us parents that our daughters would also follow in the faith of Christ. We desire that they and we may be useful in promoting and preserving the saving faith of the Lord Jesus, until He comes.

Our Own
Galatians 4:3-7

"How many children do you have?"
"We have four," I replied.
She stared curiously, then asked—
"How many are your own?"
"We have four of our own," I quietly affirmed.
"Two by birth, two by adoption;
each one lent to us by God
for a season,
to teach, to train, and love,
and then to release back to Him!"

Ours by birth or by adoption;
rights and privileges
all the same—
ours to provide and care for
while we live on earth!

Whether by birth or by adoption,
children may bring grief to parents.
But they need the assurance
of belonging,
even at their worst.
Young hearts are, oh, so tender;
how they need to know they belong.

Their parents have chosen them,
by birth or by adoption!
Thoughtless words so lightly spoken;
"How many are your own?"
cause little hearts to wonder,
"Do I belong?"
We are all adopted children,
chosen by God for His very own—
It brings a great assurance,
to know that we belong!

—Mary June Glick

Merlin & Erma Eash

Marcus — *August 7, 2001*

—Shipshewana, Indiana

The phone rang for Merlin at work. It was a call telling us we had a baby! He was born in Dover, Delaware. What a hurrying and scurrying there was! We had previously found a driver to take us, and she said she would be at our house in three hours. My sisters were at my house frantically helping me pack. At the same time, my parents were also making preparations to travel with us.

Delaware, and the time until we could hold our son in our arms, seemed so far off. We did a lot of praying and calling the agency. Upon our arrival they told us it was too late to do the paperwork and still get to the hospital. How disappointing!

Our driver suggested going to see the ocean only 45 minutes away. Standing on the beach and watching the rolling waves seemed to fit our emotions. We kept praying things would go smoothly. We met another Amish couple who had adopted two girls from Catholic Charities. They invited us to their place, which we appreciated very much.

We left for Catholic Charities to complete our paperwork. After that we waited another long five hours while they went to pick up our baby. Finally, they told us we could come and meet our son. Oh, the tears of joy that filled our eyes as we saw Marcus Wayne for the first time. After a few minutes alone with our baby, my parents also came to see him. When they saw our joy, they rejoiced with us. I took off his booties to look at his tiny feet, and he just lay there looking at me, as if he had finally found his mother. He had cried when the office staff took his booties off. We gave him his first bath and had the overwhelming feeling that this was our son whom God had added to our family.

We are very grateful for all the help Catholic Charities gave us in making this adoption possible. We also give a special thanks to our families and friends for accepting our son as our own flesh and blood. We never did meet Marcus' birthmother because we had a closed adoption, but she was a very important part of our life and our hearts. We were greatly saddened when we recently heard of her death.

Wayne & Marcia Eberly

Linford — *December 19, 1988*

Jared — *August 20, 1990*

Jana — *April 20, 1993*

—Goshen, Indiana

We are a family of five. Wayne and Marcia Eberly, Linford Jay, 14 years old, Jared Keith, 12 years, and Jana Elaine, aged 10, make up our family. We live on a Goshen, Indiana, farm. We milk around 70 dairy cows which keep us busy, plus the farming and gardening that goes with it. We attend the Wisler Mennonite Church where my father, Leonard Martin, and Marvin Ramer, are the bishops.

We've had two adoption situations working with the Department of Welfare. We took the children in foster care, then having first chance if they came up for adoption. The difficult part of that type of situation was getting attached to the children and letting go again if adoption did not come up.

We have one biological son, born to us between the other two children. They are all ours, but came in different ways. Our adopted children are born *for* us. They each have their own personality. We belong together as a family, just as families made of birth children do.

R-r-r-ring . . . "Hello. You say you have a baby for adoption."

"Yes, it is to be born a week from today and the birth-mother has decided to place it for adoption," came the reply from our social worker. I catch my breath, grab a chair, and try to relax. This can't be true, and we'd better not get our hopes up too high! A whole week to get excited and then calm ourselves down. Things like this just don't happen to us. Up and down! Up and down!

R-r-r-ring . . . Caseworker's voice! I hold my breath. "Marcia, the birthmother had her baby, but she's decided to keep it." Panic, sit down. Will it ever work out? "Wait on the Lord, be of good courage, wait I say on the Lord."

R-r-r-ring . . . Do I hear the caseworker's voice again? It is exactly one week later. Would you consider a baby for foster

Wayne Eberly family

care? I asked the first question that popped into my mind, "Is it the baby you were going to place with us for adoption?"

"Yes," she replied, "the birthmother decided she couldn't care for him." And so it is that Linford arrives to bless our home at only seven days old, and a blessing he is!

As with our other foster children, his birthmother didn't request visits. We felt threatened at times that she might. It seemed to us like a direct leading of the Lord when those visits never happened. Parental rights seemed very threatening to us. Here was the birthmother claiming rights to *our* son. But at one year of age parental rights were terminated. We had loved and cared for Linford for a whole year. Because of his special needs, the birthmother realized it was beyond her means of providing for him. Was this the Lord's way of guiding us through adoption? We were overjoyed! We did not expect an easy road ahead.

Our first hurdle was open-heart surgery at 17 months old. All went well and the hole in his heart was repaired. Our prayer remained, "Lord, make us willing to get and accept help if we need it."

Linford ended up wearing very strong glasses and hearing aids before school age. Despite the fact that we had a very special bond with him, it seemed that discipline was difficult. Disciplining him the way we had our other foster children, and the way we had been raised and taught, was not working.

We had kept contact with our caseworker, which continued to be a blessing to us. At this very difficult time she was there to coach us. She was Pentecostal, so she understood our beliefs on spanking, etc. But for Linford it was not working. "You need to get help," she said. So began our search for medical health. It has been a long road, but well worth it. At times we wondered where this would all end! But thank you to those supporters . . . special ed teachers, teachers, doctors, therapists, dentists, brothers, sisters, mom and dad who could see through him and gave encouraging words, and most of all had patience with us as parents.

A special thank you to our caseworker who thirteen years later wanted to study birthparent history to help make a diagnosis, and who miraculously found helpful information about the birthfather. Thanks to medication, Linford can be a blessing in life. Thank You, God, for doctors that are helpful and for newer medications.

Our joy at finally knowing we'd have a son without that feeling of "What if it doesn't work out?" was finally a reality! As far as having any children by birth, we had relinquished that thought some time ago. After all, we were married over five years already. Each child is made by God, according to His purpose. We already knew this; God had shown us that by the foster children we had. But it seemed like maybe God had something else to show us yet. It was to be an emotional experience; for why would God yet give us a biological son? Why didn't God give the privilege to some childless couple who hadn't crossed the adoption hurdles we had? It seemed too easy to have a child enter our family through birth. Where was the hanging on? The needing to take the child for visits, the birthparents' involvement, the court trials, the attorney's visits . . . and yet here was a child given by God with the same needs to be loved and cared for, and so Jared arrived, a child by birth. Now our family consisted of two boys 20 months apart—Linford and Jared. And with the gift, came laughter!!

R-r-r-ring . . . "Hello."

"Linford's half-sister needs foster care until she comes up for adoption. Would you be interested in giving her a home?" It didn't take long to say "yes" to taking the 7½-month-old baby. She had been neglected and didn't put weight on her feet when we tried standing her on our laps, but within several days she was standing as a normal child. She immediately won our hearts.

I did need to take her to visit her birthmother once a week. I was glad for the experience; that way I could meet her and learn to know what she's like. I always wondered what Linford's birthmother was like because she had no visits. It put me at ease, and I knew I could comfortably tell Linford and Jana they had a pleasant birthmother.

There are certain things we want to convey to our children by adoption. They need to know from little up that they are adopted. It is devastating to learn this from an outside source. Our children love to hear their adoption stories. "Mom, tell me about the day I came to live at your house." It is critical that they know their birthparents loved them, but for certain reasons were not able to provide for them. One thing that is very precious to us is that Linford was "dedicated to the Lord" before he came to our home at one week of age. Another precious thing is the request she had to have her children placed in Christian homes. Birth letters to be read to the children when they are older definitely convey that message of love. Did not Christ adopt us as His sons and daughters so we could have life?

Sometimes we are asked about "bad" adoptions? What about "bad" biological children? Sometimes we make bad choices. Satan is ever busy in all of us. There are children with special needs. We even see this in biological children. We may see special challenges more often in adopted children because of circumstances, but physical or emotional limitations are through no fault of the child or the parents. This is where adoptive parents need love and support. I guess our family doctor knew it would take a lot of encouragement. Many times we remember his words after our oldest son had been diagnosed with ADHD.

"It takes the patience of Job to work with something like

this," he kindly told me. Then he said, "The saying, 'Until you've walked a mile in his moccasins, you don't really understand' has a new meaning to me. Also, 'Father, forgive them for they know not what they say.' "

So when you say, "I pity you," don't pity us, just love and support us in knowing we are doing the best we can. Another statement we've heard is, "I could've raised that child." Have we walked where that parent walked? How is that child's brain wired? Have we encouraged them to go for help?

There are many BLESSINGS in adoption. Hearing our children say, "You're the best mom in all the world." "I love you, Mom . . . I love you, Dad!" "Mom, will you pray with me?" Precious moments!!

One hundred years from now . . .
. . . it will not matter what your bank account was,
the sort of house you lived in
or the kind of car you drove,
. . . but the world may be different
because you were important
in the life of a CHILD!

—Author Unknown

Mark Wayne & Yolanda Gascho

Wendell Mark — *November 12, 1994*

Joel Rene — *January 13, 1995*

Maribeth Joy — *December 5, 2002*

—Rutherfordton, North Carolina

Little babies always seem to attract attention, and we're trying to learn to take it in stride. This time it was the waitresses at "Pollo Campero" in Guatemala City who crowded around the table, wanting to see and hold our first-born son. While we finished our meal, they passed him from one to the other, talking to him and commenting to each other. We paid little attention to their conversation until in obvious sincerity, one of them said, "He sure looks like his father."

They'll never know what that meant to me. You see, he is not our biological child. In fact, he doesn't even have the same racial background as I do. But he is ours; one of *"the children which God hath graciously given."*

I wonder whether the full impact of Jacob's declaration (Genesis 33:5) would have come home so strongly if God had permitted us to have biological children. As newlyweds, we planned and dreamed of having a family. But the years went by and all of our planning brought us to dead-end streets. Our dreams were only dreams. God alone knew the struggles we had acknowledging and accepting that it was not His will for us to have biological children. But here, in

93

the sincere comment of a waitress was confirmation that I had become a father . . . a father by right of adoption, yet just as much a father with just as great a privilege and responsibility as if Wendell had been ours by birth.

My name is Mark Wayne Gascho and my wife is Yolanda. We have two eight-year-old sons and a daughter who is

Mark Wayne Gascho family

nearly five months old, all adopted, whom I will introduce through our story. We live in Rutherfordton, North Carolina, and are members of the Pine Ridge Mennonite Church (Nationwide Fellowship). I build custom furniture to supply the needs of our family, and serve God and the church as a minister to our local congregation.

The road that led us to adoption was not an easy road, but it was God's way for us. The first and biggest roadblock was letting go of our plans and dreams, and committing our wills to whatever God had in store for us. Then we had to learn patience as we waited for Him to reveal His will. When the opportunity finally came, we had to relearn faith. But that's getting ahead of our story.

Even before we found out that it was medically impossible for us to have children of our own, we had discussed the idea of adoption. One of my wife's friends told us that she wishes they could adopt, even though they had several biological children. To her, adoption was not second best; it was a mission with purpose—to give a Christian home and Christian upbringing to children who might otherwise grow up without parents. Adoption to her was a noble idea and it inspired us to think of it in that light. Sure, we had heard those "horror stories" of adoptive children who didn't turn out right, but we also personally knew quite a number of faithful Christian youth and adults who had been adopted. We concluded, and I believe rightly, that being naturally adopted is no more of a hurdle to being a victorious Christian than it is to be a part of a birth family. Adoptive children do have to relate to having been adopted, and we want to share more on that later.

By the time we got the doctor's verdict, we had moved back to Guatemala as missionaries. Since both of us had already spent a number of years there and we were committed to the work indefinitely, adopting in Guatemala seemed a natural choice. We communicated with a number of families who had adopted children from Guatemala and other Central American countries. Both of our families gave us their support. The way seemed clear, but where to start and how to go about it were BIG questions. Most of the children's homes in Central America run by conservative people had shut down or were no longer allowed to give children up for adoption. We checked into orphanages but returned with little hope. It seemed the only way was to do an international adoption through an adoption agency in the U.S., which we had ruled out because of the high cost. Was this another dead end?

Then one day we received word that the lawyer who did most of the mission's legal work was trying to help find a home for a baby to be born soon. The information had taken a few days to get around, and by the time we decided we were interested, a Seventh Day Adventist family had gotten their bid in first. The lawyer did offer to take our name and a phone number just in case something else came up, but she didn't sound hopeful.

A few weeks later, a widow sister from another congregation wondered whether we might be interested in adopting. She had just talked to a family friend trying to find a home for her unborn child. This time it didn't take us long to give our answer. Then the birthmother sent word that she wanted to meet us before she decided for sure. We wanted the baby, but this was a twist we hadn't planned on. We weren't too sure what we were getting into. It would be so much easier not to reckon with someone else having a vested interest in this child. We had a lot of questions, and I'm sure she did too. Up until this time, all our information had been relayed by a third party. The widow sister who had made the first contact arranged for us to meet in her home. We had to remind ourselves several times on the way over that she is just as human as we are and is just as interested in finding a good home for her child as we are in giving it one. The visit went well, and she agreed to give us the child. We understood that the baby could be born at any time and quietly went about making preparation for the eagerly expected day.

Several more weeks went by without any news. Then early one Monday morning, we got a call on the radio (we didn't have a telephone in our home). A co-worker had received a telephone call from a lawyer in the city who wanted to talk to us about an urgent matter. Since we already had plans to go to the city that morning, we decided to swing by her office.

It didn't take her long to get to the point.

"Do you want him?" she asked.

"Who? What?" The questions must have been written all over our faces even before the words came.

"Didn't the folks who took the call tell you?" she asked in surprise. "The little boy you were interested in adopting was born on Saturday. The mother made a last-minute request that he go to a couple with no children of their own, and the other couple already has several children. A friend of mine is taking care of him temporarily. Thankfully, she has a few days off work but she's wanting you to come as soon as you can to pick him up. How soon can you get there?"

We couldn't have been more astounded. Was God giving us . . . not one . . . but two?

Five days later, Wendell came home to stay.

It was nearly two months after that happy occasion that Joel was placed in our arms. We were able to hold him and take him home with us just hours after he was born.

We moved back to the U.S. just before the boys turned three. Over the intervening years, they have joined us in praying that God would make it possible for us to adopt

97

again. We decided to work through an adoption facilitator rather than an agency and do an independent adoption, since that is usually the most economical way to go. The facilitator would put us in contact with birthmothers, and we were left to develop a relationship which would hopefully result in them choosing us to be the adoptive parents for their child. Then we learned that in our society it is harder to find homes for biracial and African-American children. We determined to allow God to choose, and give us the child He would have for us.

Last December, God gave us Maribeth, a precious African-American baby girl. He sent us the news through a friend of a friend who heard of an adoption facilitator in California who had contact with a birthmother in Washington, D.C. Isn't it amazing? God's ways truly are "past finding out."

All three of our adoptions were independent national adoptions. This basically means that there was no agency involved, and we had to relate only to the adoption laws of the country (state) we were living in at the time. We had to have home studies done and all that goes with it, and we needed to hire attorneys to take care of the legal work.

The first two were done in Guatemala. Since we did not do an international adoption, we had to have the boys in our care for two full years before they became eligible for visas. However, at the end of the two years, the U.S. government considered them ours, and we were exempted from the international adoption requirements that we would otherwise have had to meet.

We did learn that it pays to do some homework and find a lawyer up on adoption laws and acquainted with all the legal procedures. One of our lawyers was two steps ahead of the system all the way through, while the other was learning as she went. The suspense and uncertainty of not knowing the process is bad enough without having to deal with a lawyer who doesn't know either.

Here in the U.S. we signed up with an adoption facilitator called *The LINK*. They are based here in North Carolina and are pretty much staffed by volunteers, most of whom are either adoptive parents or birthmothers who have given up children in adoption. They advertise their services to birthmothers through ads in the yellow pages, newspaper ads, ads in baby and parenting magazines, websites, and multimedia. When a birthmother contacts them, they interview her to make sure her story is reasonable. They then send the birthmother to the website for a brief description of the families considering adoption, or send her a portfolio of color pictures made up by each family to depict what life would be like in their home. The birthmother is allowed to choose which families she would like to interview or which she may be interested in learning more about. She is then put in contact with those families and the final decision is up to her. The facilitator serves mostly as a sounding board from this point on, but is available to recommend attorneys and discuss procedures. *The LINK* does have a strong religious emphasis and requires that each prospective adoptive couple sign a statement of belief along with their pastor before they will accept an application. They do make housing available for the birthmothers, and, if needed, try to help them find jobs or get education.

Doing an independent adoption does require that the adoptive parents work closely with the birthparents at every step of the process. Birthparents want the best for their children, but somehow have been convinced that they cannot give them what they really need. Letting them know we would love to have their child as a part of our family, without putting undue pressure on them to give it up, can be a real challenge. Many times they are trying to deal with broken homes, unfaithful partners, dependent children, and the guilt of sinful living. Developing the kind of relationship that will help them is a real challenge. We wonder at times whether some of our "failed" relationships were God's way of putting people who are seeking in touch with His ambassadors. It can be very stressful at times, but we have found it an opportunity to share our faith in God with those we have come to know. May God help us to be faithful.

Then there is also the matter of resolving how much contact there will be between birthparents and adoptive families. There is a push in our society for open adoptions, which means that, while the child becomes a part of his/her adoptive family, they still retain close ties to their birthparents. The birthparents may even have a right to make some decisions in relation to the child. This is a matter that needs to be carefully considered and aired early in the relationship.

We have appreciated and needed the support of our extended family and church group in our adoption journey. Their prayers and encouragement have been so much help. Their acceptance of our children has made it easy for us to forget they are adopted.

Several things we have learned in relation to adoption and our children:

It is important that we deal with our feelings about wanting biological children. God created us (especially women) with a yearning to experience parenthood. This is God's plan and it is natural and right. To deny this desire or try to pretend it really doesn't matter, works against God's plan for the family. To turn our interest to special pets is not the answer. We do need to find a way to express and exercise these feelings even while we are working through them and trying to find God's will for us in childlessness. We were encouraged to involve ourselves in relating to other children. It helps. Volunteer to baby-sit for your extended family, for that busy young mother, or when someone is sick. Visit school. Take time for children after church. Teach Sunday school when you are asked. Hold babies even though it is hard to do. You will likely find yourself having to cry it out many times over. This is natural. Dealing with these feelings is not something you can do once or twice and put it all behind. God would not have it that way. He loves children and wants us to love them too. He also loves us and wants the best for us.

Don't isolate yourself. Satan would have us think no one understands; that no one *can* understand. Listen. We need each other. We need our brethren and sisters in the church. Find someone to share with—your parents, another couple who has already faced the challenge, your ministry and their wives, or another trustworthy Christian friend. Bottling it up makes it very difficult to deal with. Sharing lightens the load.

Our children will deal with adoption in much the same way we deal with it. Adoption dare not be considered second best. If God has called you to it, then it is the best. Our children are not ours because we couldn't have biological children; they are ours because God gave them to us. Any other reason is not reason enough and is bound to have repercussions in the life and thought processes of the child.

We do not want our children to remember when they found out they were adopted. Not that we make an issue of it, but it seems to be much easier to relate to than an adoption that is hidden until the child is a teenager or beyond. We made it a point to tell our children about their adoption even before we were sure they could understand. It does raise some questions which need to be answered with propriety and honesty, but it prepares them to relate realistically to their past. At the same time, we do not make this an object of discussion with every person who asks. When confronted with the casual question, "Are these your children?"

the answer is "Yes" and not "They're adopted." If someone specifically asks about adoption we answer truthfully. We seldom think of them being adopted unless someone stops us with a question. We do well to reinforce in our children's minds and in our own that we are one family, regardless of our background.

You will need to prepare yourselves for the looks, the question mark expressions, and the thoughtless comments of people who do not understand your situation. They will happen and often they will hurt. Remember that if you are in God's will, there is no temptation that does not have an escape route. You may need to bite your lip or walk away, but God's grace is sufficient for acceptance and forgiveness.

If you decide that God would have you adopt, don't wait for a child to appear. Begin your paperwork. Plan for finances. Make the necessary connections. Do all you know to do, but don't forget to leave it in God's hands. Pray often that He would direct your contacts and your relationships and leave it with Him. He may take you into situations that do not work out. Don't push to make it work your way. God has a purpose for these too, that we often cannot see at the time. It is a blessing to be able to look back and see God working out the details for each child He gives you.

10

Daryl & Naomi Lehman

Brittney Joy — *August 3, 2002*

—Shipshewana, Indiana

We are happy to share our adoption story and of the joy we have experienced since the adoption of our little girl, Brittney Joy. We, Daryl and Naomi Lehman, belong to the Amish church. Daryl is a lawn irrigation contractor and runs his own business. I am a stay-at-home mom (finally!). I waited 6½ years for this dream to come true. I worked as a waitress after we married in May of 1996, each year thinking surely this will be my last year at work as a waitress. God knew what His plans were for us, and we tried to be patient. We went through disappointing fertility treatments in hopes to conceive, but with no results and no answers as to why we weren't able to conceive.

I mentioned the idea of adoption, but Daryl just didn't think he was ready at the time to make that step. I tried to forget it, but always in the back of my mind, I wanted to adopt a baby. I started baby-sitting part-time to keep my mind occupied with other things. Daryl and I got so attached to these children, we knew if we adopted a child, we would have no less love for the child than if we had a baby by birth.

Now that the decision was made, we knew this is what we wanted to do. We felt this was God's choice for us to create our family. Norman and Karen Mast came over one evening to share the stories of their two children. They encouraged

103

us greatly, and we were pretty excited to get started the next morning. Taking the step into the unknown seemed overwhelming.

We started calling and shopping around for agencies and facilitators. It was hard deciding which way to go. Agencies as a rule are against facilitators, and vice versa, so talking to one then the other made it very confusing.

Agencies are more expensive to a certain extent, but they do a lot more work for you. Facilitators can become expensive if a couple cases fall through and living expenses, etc., have already been paid.

After receiving recommendations from other couples, we decided to go with Silver Spoon Adoption from California. We had barely started our home study when we got our first roller-coaster-ride call, the "up" of thinking we're getting a baby to the "down" of it not working out. After five of these calls in a 10-month time span, it was more than we could handle, and we asked them not to call us any more.

We contracted with Lifetime Facilitation Center from California. The contract with Lifetime had to be paid when we were ready to start, then it would be good for two years. They required 30 profiles of Daryl and me to begin with to hand out to potential birthmoms. The information we received about them through a friend seemed very reputable, and they are nice to work with. The profiles were a lot of work, but we were sure they would be worth it if we got a baby. After 11 months with them and still no leads, we were a little on the impatient side again when we met with Norm and Karen Mast on Sunday evening, July 28.

They were excited to announce they had been matched with a birthmom again. This would be their third child through Silver Spoon. They really seemed to have good results with them. After spending the evening talking about adoption and babies, our hearts were pumping full tilt for a baby.

Not knowing what a call to Silver Spoon would result in, but trusting God would lead us to the right baby in His timing, I called Silver Spoon Monday morning, July 29. When I talked with Jennifer, she was very positive she could have a baby for us in a couple months. This was very exciting for us, yet it seemed unreal to try and imagine us being a mommy and daddy in a couple months!

On Monday, August 5, 2002, I was in my normal routine of doing laundry and working outside. At 8:00 a.m. I decided to check my messages. Lifetime is located in California, three hours behind us, but there was a message and it was from Silver Spoon! "Hi! This is Jennifer at Silver Spoon. I have a baby girl born on August 3rd. If you are interested call me at 909-764-2445." I ran for the phone booth and called and called, but I just couldn't get through. After trying her other number and no answer, I was getting pretty frustrated.

I called Daryl to see what he thought. He said, "Keep trying!" He was so excited. We both knew time was of the essence in dealing with Jennifer. I called Karen Mast, who had Jennifer's daughter's phone number. "Try her!" she said. Lisa answered and was very excited to hear from us. Jennifer had told her she would call us about the baby and she was expecting to hear from us. Lisa said she would put us on the case.

The reason we couldn't reach Jennifer was because she was flying from her home in southern California to northern California where the baby was born. The infant was being released from the hospital that day, August 5, and if Jennifer would not have been there to receive her, state foster care would have stepped in.

Unknown to Lisa, Daryl, and I, Jennifer had also notified another couple about the baby, and they had returned her call before she got on the plane, so Jennifer had them on the case also. Monday night we received a call from Jennifer saying, "Sorry, but the other couple will have first chance since they returned the call first."

We were very let down again! It was hard to pray, "Thy will be done." I told Daryl, "If it's supposed to work out for us, it will, in God's timing. We will just have to be patient."

Tuesday, August 6th, dawned a sunny summer morning, and I was in pretty good spirits again and set to work outside. It was a normal busy day. By afternoon a call from Jennifer changed the whole day. She said she talked to Lisa, and to be fair, they should let the birthmom choose after presenting both of us. I called Daryl immediately to see what he would say and he was overjoyed, as I was. We still had a chance.

Jennifer called about an hour later to say, "She is yours." The birthmom chose us as she preferred someone without other children, and she also thought it was a special "omen" that the baby was born on my birthday. I thought that was so special that she was born on my birthday.

Plans were made that afternoon to fly out Wednesday morning. We arrived in Ontario, California, airport in the early evening, California time. Since the situation was a little different than usual with Jennifer having the baby at her house instead of us picking the baby up at the hospital, we went to Jennifer's house first thing from the airport to greet our little girl. Jennifer handed her to Daryl first, then he handed her to me. Oh, what a feeling of love and joy! We can hardly put into words how wonderful it was to hold our baby for the first time! We named her Brittney Joy.

Jennifer welcomed us to stay at her house till the paperwork was done. We thought it was very generous of her to let us stay there at no cost instead of getting a hotel. We were most glad to hear the words, "You may go home." There's nothing like "Home, Sweet Home" when you've lived with strangers for a week.

We really feel we had a great experience with the adoption of Brittney Joy. It brought us so close to God, knowing that only through His will and guidance was all this possible. We put our full trust in Him to pull us through the rough times.

We feel very fortunate that Naomi got to talk with the birthmom on the phone. Our feelings toward birthparents did a turnaround since we have gone through the adoption process. Our hearts really go out to these mothers. So often we are asked, "How could she?! How could any woman give up her child?"

Our answer, "It takes an unselfish and courageous woman to give up a child she cannot care for, and it takes precious little character to get an abortion instead."

These mothers are so special to us, and we really care about them. I think of Brittney's birthmom every day and pray for her. I hope we were able to explain how thankful we are to her in the letter we wrote her when we got home. We also sent pictures of Brittney and us in hopes it would comfort her.

I think it would be challenging to not have support from family and friends. Our families on both sides fully accepted Brittney and our decision to adopt which we are so thankful for.

"Wishing to all, God's Blessings!"

Some Would Gather Money

Some would gather money
Along the path of life,
Some would gather roses,
And rest from worldly strife.

But we would gather children
With gladness bring them in.
We would seek bright, sparkling eyes,
And a carefree, toothless grin.

For money cannot enter
In the land of endless day.
And the roses that are gathered,
Soon will wilt and fade away.

But oh, the laughing children,
As we cross the sunset sea.
And the gates swing wide to heaven
They are our eternal legacy!

Written by Mary Jane Proft.
Reprinted with permission of *Mary Sue Originals*.

11

Judy Martin

Corey Grant — *May 20, 1986*

—Goshen, Indiana

"Suffer little children to come unto me, and forbid them not: for of such is the Kingdom of God."

What a privilege it is to be able to love a child! The innocence and the trust they put in you shows us how God wants us to trust Him with all our hearts—to hold nothing back! We have to become as little children.

I am single and always loved children! I have a saying on my wall—"My day is complete. I saw a child smile!" How true! I had the opportunity to take care of a 3-week-old baby for a single mother that had worked for us in previous years at the restaurant. When the baby was 14 months old, her mother and father married and moved to California. What an empty spot this left in my life! I then began thinking of foreign adoptions, thinking it might be easier since I was single. My dad then suggested I try foster parenting first. My son, Corey, was the first and only foster child I had other than having a few children for a weekend. Corey came into my home at the age of nine months. He was asthmatic and had been in the hospital eight times. Because of neglect he was unable to sit, but by the time he was twelve months, he had caught up to his peers. What energy! He was going to make up for all he had missed! I spent many nights sitting up in bed holding him so he could breathe. I carried a breathing machine for him with me to work. By the time he was four years old, he had totally outgrown his asthma. He has not been to the doctor since for an illness. We have been blessed! We know though that it is in God's hands and with His strength we can make it no matter what is placed in front of us if we lean on Him for our strength and not on our own. I have proof that through my own strength, we can't make it.

Every Saturday until Corey was five and one-half years old he went for birthparent visits. Home visits became bad enough that the judge changed the visits to be supervised at Child Protective Services. Two weeks before he turned six, I was able to adopt him.

Single parenting without proper support is a disaster. I

Judy Martin family

am a member of the Yellow Creek Wisler Mennonite Church. Corey went to our church school, Harrison Christian School. I cannot express the support I had from his teachers. God bless them! They spent extra hours mornings before school, and even some evenings, to give me a break. Family support is also a must. Corey and my dad were very close. God's ways are so much higher than ours, and on this side of heaven we will never understand it all, but He saw fit to take my dad home. We found out he had a brain tumor, and he died two months later. Corey was six. Life turned into a struggle financially and spiritually for me. Corey went from baby-sitter to baby-sitter (mostly family) while I worked 60-65-hour weeks. Corey craved male attention, and in my family the men all had children and many responsibilities of their own. Finally I was able to get a job at a feed mill as secretary for my brother-in-law, which made it possible to have Corey go to work with me. Corey began choring evenings for a young married man in our church, and he is still very important to him. Thanks, Andrew!

By this time Corey was in the upper grades and was struggling with where he belonged. Our communication deteriorated as both of us were frustrated. One evening, Chief Dave from Bald Eagle Wilderness Camp in Pennsylvania came to our school and showed slides of camp. I went, thinking I might get some advice. The presentation was mainly on what camp was about. I went away thinking that it was something I couldn't afford. Corey thought camp sounded interesting—but not for him.

Things kept on going downhill, until one day I decided to make the call. I remember I was shaking and could hardly say what I needed. I thought they would surely think I was a basket case! I remember talking to Chief Mark, and he seemed so calm and reassuring that I began to feel hope. He told me they only take boys that want to come. The boy had to say yes

111

to coming to camp. I was also told there was a waiting list.

I filled out the application they sent, and my family lovingly gave us the financial support. Family is very important. I waited seven months until Chief Mark came for a home visit. He brought along a photo album of camp. Corey, of course, was not interested in any of it. (Now we have five albums!) This visit wasn't for Corey to decide if he wanted to go to camp, but if he was willing to come for a visit. Camp is a place that you can feel the love and dedication the chiefs have for the boys. They are under a very organized Christian atmosphere. Camp is a place where it is okay to have problems, which enables them to work through them. I just want to thank them for the time and effort they take to help the boys. It takes special people.

We went for a visit, and again God was in control. Corey agreed to go to camp. Camp did not make him think it would be easy, but he said yes anyway. I remember waiting for him to answer, and I was afraid of a yes or a no. I don't know how to express the feeling of putting your child in a tent in the middle of the winter and going home and crawling into your own warm bed. I went through the struggle of what I would have felt like if my dad had done this to me. It hurt! Camp is usually 18 months to two years. And this seemed like a long time. But nineteen months later and 38 trips to Pennsylvania, we are through camp.

I just want you to know there is help, and camp was such a blessing to Corey and me just in learning how to communicate and in a lot of other things, such as who needs to be in control. Camp is not only for the adopted, but for anyone who has problems to work through. Camp is a good place for boys to learn about nature and themselves.

They have two rules and that is to do everything together and with a good attitude. That is a challenge for all of us. You know, I have often sat in a group with people talking

112

about this problem child or adult, and that, well, he or she was an adopted child. If you stop to think, you can probably name as many birth children with problems as you can adopted. I have heard these discussions take place right in front of the adopted. Are we not all adopted into God's family? We weren't born into it. Why were we so blessed to be the ones born in a free country or a Christian home? Was it our choice? What is our Christian attitude towards those who haven't had those privileges? What is our duty? Why were we chosen? Are we abusing the blessings and the opportunities given us? Words can hurt, and we all have struggles.

Should singles adopt? I've been blessed! Would I encourage other singles? Is it easy? No. Would Corey think it is a good idea? This was his answer: "IF the mother can be at home and the child knows where he is going to be. But, not knowing where you're going or where your place is, is very hard!" There are a lot of abused and neglected children. What is our responsibility? Let us seek God's will and let Him direct us. I think children need a two-parent home, but you know that sometimes God even calls one of them home. I just ask that you keep praying for us. Our struggles are not over, and they won't be till God calls us home.

Corey is now 17 and home from camp to stay. He has accepted Christ, and the devil does not like the light in us, so he is ever out there to discourage us to put darkness into us, but with God's help we will win! Being a woman, maybe a girl would have been easier at this age, because Corey does need a man. But, thank God, I have a son! I did not give birth to Corey, but I cannot imagine loving a birth child more.

My heart aches for people that doubt this, because God's love goes so far and so deep for everyone of us! Can you feel it? Have you been adopted into His family? Someday, all of us that are adopted into His family will be over there in mansions with streets of gold, sitting at Jesus' feet! We are ALL adopted.

113

Father, Hear Us, We Are Praying

Father, hear us, we are praying.
Hear the words our hearts are saying.
We are praying for our children.
Keep them from the powers of evil,
From the secret, hidden peril,
Father, hear us, for our children.
From the whirlpool that would suck them,
From the treacherous quicksand, pluck them.
Father, hear us, for our children.
From the worldling's hollow gladness,
From the sting of faithless sadness,
Father, Father, keep our children.
Through life's troubled waters steer them,
Through life's bitter battles cheer them.
Father, Father, be Thou near them.
Read the language of our longing,
Read the wordless pleadings thronging.
Holy Father, for our children,
And wherever they may bide,
Lead them Home at eventide.

—Amy Carmichael

12

Lydia Martin

Stephen — *February 14, 1976 d. January 20, 1999*
Jolene — *August 26, 1983*

—Ephrata, Pennsylvania

I am a single foster and adoptive parent to two children, one of whom has already gone to his heavenly home. I am a member of Martindale Mennonite Church. As a young school girl, I remember I used to think I'd like children, but I wasn't sure if I'd want to be married. God was already molding me for my life's mission. I worked in a hospital as a nursing assistant and saw many needy children. This prompted me to become a foster parent. I pursued this route, but at that time they were not very open to single foster parents. I was disappointed, but God had other plans. In February 1976, I was working in the nursery at the hospital, and out of the clear blue, a doctor walked in and said, "I think you should adopt a child." He didn't even know me that well. He said he would give me the name of an agency through which they adopted—Tressler Lutheran Social Services in York.

I had a very good experience with them in doing my home study. I strongly felt something would turn up not allowing me to do this, but it didn't; it was all in God's plan.

The first child referred to me was a little boy with cystic fibrosis. This problem I had decided I probably could not handle. God made concrete what my answer would be. Shortly after, a little 16-month-old boy was referred. I took

115

one look at his picture and said, "That's my boy!" The foster parents asked me what I would name him. When I said, "Stephen," they said, "we thought you would name him that." Message from God! My advice to other potential adoptive parents is, totally put it in God's hands. He will

Lydia Martin family

guide your steps to adoption if this is His plan for you.

In 1981, I finally became approved to do foster care. I worked part-time at the hospital also, so I was very busy, but not too busy to listen when I was told there are two baby girls available for adoption who have Down's syndrome. I was told I would get first chance because the other interested family already had adopted a child with Down's syndrome. Again, this was God's plan, I'm sure. The other baby had lots of heart surgeries, where my daughter was healthy. It would have been very hard for me to spend a lot of time in the hospital. At the time I adopted, single persons were only allowed to adopt special needs children. This has changed, although I have no doubt that these two children were the ones God wanted me to have.

Stephen, my son, was 18 months old when I received him into my home, and Jolene, my daughter, was six weeks. During all this time, I also was doing foster care. In 1989, I finally quit my part-time job and became a full-time foster and adoptive mother, working mostly with medically involved children.

In 1992, a little girl whom I had kept for four years passed away from a malignant brain tumor. Nine months later another little girl, 14 months old, died suddenly in a respite home, while I was in the hospital for surgery. In January 1999, my adopted son Stephen became very ill, and in six weeks' time he also died of a malignant brain tumor. Stephen had special needs, and I often concerned myself about who would care for him when I no longer could. It was all in God's plan that He would take him in His tender arms and care for him till I can join him again. Again, I say, "Put your trust in Him." He knows it all from beginning to end.

Some advice I would like to give is to talk to your children about adoption as generally as you would any other subject, and do it from day one. Answer questions honestly and as simply as possible. When they are ready for more, they will ask.

Support from family, church, and schools is also very important. I feel one must move slowly at times till full acceptance of adoption is attained. And when identifying your children to others don't say, "These are adopted, and these are our birth children." They are simply "our children" and no different if by adoption or by birth.

I Asked God . . .

I asked God to take away my habit.
God said, No.
It is not for me to take away, but for you to give it up.

I asked God to make my handicapped child whole.
God said, No.
His spirit is whole; his body is only temporary.

I asked God to grant me patience.
God said, No.
Patience is a by-product of tribulations;
It isn't granted, it is learned.

I asked God to give me happiness.
God said, No.
I give you blessings; happiness is up to you.

I asked God to spare me pain.
God said, No.
Suffering draws you apart from worldly cares
And brings you closer to Me.

I asked God to make my spirit grow.
God said, No.
You must grow on your own!
But I will prune you to make you fruitful.

I asked God for all things that I might enjoy in life.
God said, No.
I will give you life, so that you may enjoy all things.

I asked God to help me LOVE others,
As much as He loves me.
God said, . . . Ahhh, finally you have the idea.

—Author Unknown

13

Joe & Arlene Mast

Nathan, Crystal, Nathanael, Wanda, Jimmie

— *Arlene's first marriage*

John William Andrew — *June 17, 1989*

Marina Jolene — *December 13, 1993*

Natalia Arlene — *October 7, 1997*

Ruslin Joseph — *January 25, 1999*

—Amelia, Virginia

Journal or biography notes in italics.

Jim and Arlene Toms were blessed with five children—Nathan, Crystal, Nathanael, Wanda, and Jimmie. After Jim's death, Arlene remained a widow for nine years. That's when I, Joe Mast, became acquainted with Arlene and her children. After about eight months of courtship, we were married on March 15, 1997. It was my first marriage. I was 43 years old and she was 45.

We had a goal to finish raising our children in an environment they would enjoy and could develop in. We wanted them to remember this new home as home. We wanted them to mature in their Christian lives and serve Christ. We wanted them to be spared of the many hardships and disappointments that sinful living brings. We wanted them to heal from past disappointments and emotional trauma, and the death of their father, and to learn valuable lessons from it. We wanted them to respect their birthfather and to learn to love me as a dad.

And we wanted more children. We knew there were children with needs, and we needed children. Our children needed them too. But God saw differently at first. Arlene had a miscarriage. I had mononucleosis. We just couldn't go ahead with anything for a while. Later we wanted three children from the Bethel placement center in Romania spread out over a year. But the Romania orphanage was always just about ready for us to work on a child from there, but never quite.

Joe Mast family

Arlene wrote: *"Joe and I were really wishing for children of our own. The miscarriage was a disappointment for the whole family, but we knew God knew best. [Especially] since then we've been wishing to adopt. At first I wasn't so sure about it but then I became very excited about it and we're so hoping God will grant our wish for two little children. Our children are the only things we can take to heaven with us."*

Our quest for a child may have formally started January 8, 2000. But it was February 2001 when we were finally asked to send an application to Joe Miller, Seymour, MO. In March we were finally informed that things just were not working out and that we should go elsewhere. Arlene was 48 at the time, and we were concerned that time was running out.

He Shall Be Called "Johnny." On March 1, 2000, we received a call from Faith Mission Home, in Virginia, a retarded children's home, asking us if we knew anyone that could take a ten-year-old boy. He had been placed there in

Joe and Arlene Mast extended family

desperation by his dad (uncle) and he really didn't fit in there. The staff all hated for John to go back to his home situation and his dad wanted something better for him. Taking a bundle of emotions into our custody looked huge. But hadn't we been praying for a child? This was from such an unexpected angle and age! We considered telling the dad we could take the pressure off him for the weekend. But we couldn't do that to the dad. Then we considered taking him for the summer. But that is having a child that doesn't really belong, and didn't fix the problem of him having to be moved. But to say, "We will take him," is so final. It is like getting married. And how would this affect our ability to acquire other children?

Well, two days after we got that call, we had a boy in our home. We called him Johnny. His dad brought him and all his belongings, which wasn't much. We went shopping for shoes and clothes right away. This was just a bit stressful to Arlene. Changes were coming a little too fast.

Johnny wanted very much to please us and soon learned what we expected of him, usually responding before we were done talking. So he usually did only the first thing we said, and even now, three years later, he has a hard time taking directions if more than one thing is to be done. His coordination was poor. He could not concentrate. He could not relate a happening in a way that we could understand. Any noise or movement would distract him from schoolwork. We taught him at home in the summer, trying to get him to fit into a grade in school.

Johnny walked slightly bowed with his eyes looking at his feet. Finally we got him evaluated by Joan Martin from Pennsylvania. After ninth months of patterning and other exercises, he had improved so much that we stopped the program. But learning remains hard for him, and he has some trouble with seizures. The possibility of a seizure rules out

124

driving tractors, mowers, or motorbikes. He is a terrific swimmer, but must always wear a life preserver

Our very familiar friends all knew about Johnny, but there were people we would meet at church meetings or in our travels that would have questions about who exactly Johnny was, perhaps knowing we got married recently but little else. Once after a service a slight acquaintance observed, "I've been watching you and I can't quite figure this out. Is he your dad or are you just staying with him or what?" I overheard the question and knew Johnny would have difficulty answering it. I moved toward the two even as Johnny moved toward me. My reply was an effort to ease the situation for all three of us. I said, "Johnny came into our home March 3, and he has brought a lot of sunshine into our home."

On another occasion one of Arlene's former acquaintances had a question. He knew just enough to have a bit of a problem. Johnny looked like the family. Actually, you can hardly tell the difference from pictures of Nathanael when he was Johnny's age. Both have red hair and freckles. Johnny was too young to be from Arlene's former marriage. He seemed too old to be from our recent marriage. They had been of the opinion (rightly) that I had no children before my marriage to Arlene, but were ready to doubt it now. So he asked that old question, "Is he yours?" The question simply meant who donated this child to the family—I, Arlene and Jim, or Arlene and I. Now, the answer "no" would have fixed it up for him and me, but not for a wide-eyed boy of 10, hoping he belonged. Again I said that he came March 3rd and brought a lot of sunshine into our home.

In April 2001, we went to the court and requested custody of Johnny. It went really well. We try to keep the visits to his birthmother to once or twice a year. He does see his uncle, whom he called Dad, more often, as he is in the area.

His aunt has since divorced his uncle and never makes contact. His birthfather is deceased.

Ever since the coming of Marina, Natalia, and Ruslin in February 2002, Johnny has many questions. He wants to be adopted, but doesn't understand it all and is somewhat afraid of it. I explain that his uncle will always be his birthuncle and he will have so many more uncles. He often discusses who his (new) cousins, nephews, grandparents, and nieces are, as if he treasures it. The adoption discussion has moved from the bedtime goodnight conversations to the dinner table. I think that is progress.

Our Changing Concepts. Finally we felt ready to move ahead with other adoption plans. We attended an adoption orientation in Richmond, sponsored by a Catholic agency. Perhaps a Christian-based agency might be Mennonite-friendly. We were made a bit more aware of the requirements, restrictions, and costs and how they varied from country to country. International adoption seemed the way to go for several reasons. A child who goes through the welfare system in the U.S. is often exposed to many detrimental things. And since our ages were what they were, we figured getting an infant was almost impossible. Orphanages in other countries are poor, but simple, some without the TV. And maybe we could get an infant. We thought the cultural shock would be less for such a child than one who has been into everything here in the States. We now preferred two children, a boy and a girl, perhaps one and two years old or as young as possible.

Getting Started. In May 2001, we finally contacted the agency that Bethel Placement Center in Romania used—Carolina Adoption Agency in Greensboro, NC—and things started moving. *We paid the $150 registration, and met reps for a number of countries. Romania, China, and Ukraine have very good orphanages. Referrals are made after you get into the country,* but you can refuse the referral and request another. There is usually a long in-country stay. Russian adoptions are more certain to involve healthy children. Ukraine stands out ahead for us right now, Russia being a possibility, and Romania seems to be coming along. China has many girls, but boys are very rare.

Home Study and Documentation. Since we had to do our home study in Virginia, we were referred to ABC Adoption Services in Roanoke. On May 8, 2001, we had our INTAKE STUDY, paid $65.00, and attended an informative meeting on international adoptions in the evening. *All seems well except for the requirement to sign not to use corporal punishment. We called Tanya in NC. She said she will talk with Ann Carpenter at ABC to try to work something out.*

The home study was much like going to college. We thought the assignments were huge. We were to start paperwork as soon as possible, so the country of origin had to be chosen. There were many reports and forms. Arlene and I had to write our life stories, using a very extensive outline. They were to be 16 pages long each and include everything from birth to school to attitudes toward parents and their methods of training and what our feelings were about everything, all the way up to our marriage and attitudes and daily schedules and thoughts on the future. Later, when in Russia, the lady judge was quite concerned and questioned us extensively about how we relate to nonmembers and doctors and who we lived around and what the children would be allowed to do, etc. We were told that our life stories were 90% religious and she was apprehensive!

Our evening classes ran each Friday in June. We were instructed how to (and not to) respond to many types of behavior. The classes that zeroed in on child training tasted like they came out of magazines such as *Parents*. We were told not to be consistent because we can't be! Also parents shouldn't agree on everything because that is like two adults

127

ganging up on a child! You are supposed to allow the child to move up to adulthood with almost no interference. You become a facilitator and nudge the child in the way he wants to go. In a nutshell, if you handle any situation in a way that takes the control away from the child to put you as the parent in control, or it appears to the child that you do so, you supposedly respond incorrectly.

Overall though, the home study was good for us. We became more aware of the special needs of orphans. Almost every possible eventuality was examined. We became open to our own shortcomings and needs. I am more a person who knows there will be obstacles, but God will see us through if we are dedicated to getting through and have faith in Him.

The agency helped us file the correct papers to the correct places at the correct time. How would we have known where and when to get criminal background checks, medical checks, and all with properly notarized, apostilled documentation? Where would we have sent these documents? Where could we have found the right courier services in Washington? Yes, and how would it feel, if we would have ever gotten to Russia, to find that some paper was missing or defective in Russia's eyes and we would come home without the children?

One little problem we had was in relation to swearing or taking the oath. There were no problems with any American institutions such as immigration, embassies, state police, etc. But some of the documents were going to Russia. The agency had forms they used for years and believed they could not be changed. They didn't want to make a problem with any of the Russian officials who were getting these documents. Over the years they got a sense of what the Russians like. But really there are three basic notary forms for three different applications. If the form indicates that the notary vouches for the document, he does the swearing or affirming, or if we affirmed instead of swearing we had no problem with it. But if the wording had us swearing, generally I would cross out "swear" and write in "affirm." But what would the Russians think?

Seeing this reluctance to changing the forms, I consulted a local lawyer. He said, "Affirming is accepted in the courts of law and no one else should have a problem with it." Another source sent me the wordings of the three basic forms. So I just spent some time on my computer and rewrote all the offending documents so we wouldn't have to cross out anything. Why swear when the Word says, "Above all things, my brethren, swear not"? I believe this issue was new to Ann and she had a problem with any changes, but finally allowed them.

Also there was the question of swearing in the Russian court. I was concerned that the Russians would not look kindly on a change of form. We intended to talk to our court advocate on the first trip over, so that the judge would be forewarned. We found out that Russia, being an atheistic country, does not require swearing at all. We just had to say we would tell the truth. Can you imagine an atheist placing his hand on the Bible or raising his hand to heaven? I wondered if they might sometimes swear by Lenin or Peter the Great. In old times God was pleased when men swore by His name instead of by heathen gods.

Sensing God's Leading for Our Little Gifts. There were certain things important to us in choosing the country and the type of children. We did want a boy and girl. We hardly felt we should take a special needs child at our age and with Johnny's problems. Our desire was that the Lord lead in this. We did not want to say no to a child He wanted us to have.

On one of our trips to ABC Adoption Services in

Roanoke, we knew we would be seeing pictures of a group of three siblings—a boy (6), a girl (8), and a girl (10) from Russia. Ann Carpenter really encouraged us to take them. She told us to go home and think about it. This was quite different from what we originally decided. Could we handle three instead of two? Was this the Lord's will? Should we stick to what we thought was the Lord's will? Is this child-shopping? We were concerned about the exposure to unwholesome things in that many older children. The pictures were sweet. The children were saying poems and dancing in front of a Christmas tree. After much prayer and consideration we decided to tell her if she could just turn the ages down a little it would be better. But we asked the Lord to please make His will known in such a way we would not reject any child on our own.

We were then told of another sibling group nearly the same—a boy (2), a girl (3), and another girl (7). We went to Roanoke with mixed feelings, wondering how this would turn out.

When we got there we saw pictures of this group and were drawn to them immediately. But the pictures of the other three children were still somewhat in our minds, and still are today, a year and a half later. Ann then told us that it was doubtful she could get the first group as the area was temporarily closed to adoptions. This was the answer we prayed for.

Others' Attitudes. One of our concerns was how the adoption agency personnel felt about our way of life and placing children in our Christian home. There were several horror stories in the plain churches where the social services seemed to step way out of line. I asked Ann Carpenter with ABC Adoption if she thought there would be a problem with a seven-year-old girl adapting to our culture. Her response? "Don't you worry. That girl will be Daddy's girl.

She'll do well in your home. You live back in the woods where you can control her contacts and exposure exactly the way you want. You can release her to church people and acquaintances. They are very restricted in Russia and so are more able to adapt to you than the regular run of my clients. Why, Arlene will stay home and you aren't even talking about day care!" Later in answer to a similar question, Ann Huntingdon from Carolina Adoption responded with: "No worry at all. You don't even have TV, which is a plus. I wish all our clients gave me as little worry as you and Arlene. You're kid people." So much for wondering if they were just putting up with us.

As for others' attitudes toward our adopting, Arlene wrote: "*It is very interesting to see the reaction of friends and family when they find out about us adopting. Some want us to go right away and get a child, but we tell them it takes time! They are all happy for us, but we haven't told very many outside our family. We sort of wanted to surprise people, but probably when we take our trips, we won't be able to as much. We have enough friends that have adopted that we will have good support and encouragement from them.*"

Preparing for the First Trip. Many documents were prepared before our first trip. Some went to American immigration, some to social services, some to places in Russia. Many papers had to be properly notarized and apostilled. The apostille is the state validation. We also had to have a letter of invitation from Russia to even go. All this was coordinated by the placing agency and the adoption agency.

Suddenly we had a travel date! And suddenly there wasn't enough time to get all the medical documents and other paperwork done, visas and tickets gotten, things lined up at home, etc.

Remember, we started the home study in June 2001 and now we were already leaving for the first trip in November.

131

We left on a Monday and came back on Saturday. Not many folks knew anything about this—just family, close friends, ministers who had to sign papers or vouch for us, and certain others who had to be involved.

After landing in Moscow, we went through immigration with another couple. Stepping out of the line toward a glass wall and hall, we were met by Mr. Oleg's people, Sergei, our interpreter, and his son, Stepon, our driver. We recognized them from pictures shown us during our travel orientation at Carolina Adoptions. Also they had their IDs on. We were carrying large amounts of money, and, believe it or not, were eager to get rid of it.

Stepon expertly maneuvered the car through the Moscow traffic to a little drive on the backside of some high-rise apartments. We went into a bleak building, entered a small corridor with a mini elevator that took us to another floor. There we found some carpeted rooms and a bathroom. And there we unloaded lots of US 100-dollar bills from various hiding places.

Soon we were rushed to a regional airport, given excellent directions, passed through the security, and were on our own in a very strange world. Moving down the hall, we turned where we were told, looking back at friendly nodding faces for assurance. When everyone else went down the stairs, we went along. On the tarmac were two buses. I said "Ulianovsk" to the officer by the first one and she ushered us in. We drove in between planes in a huge parking lot and stopped behind one of them. The steps went up under the tail. We deposited our luggage just inside the plane, as a man stowed them, and proceeded to the front of the almost-full plane.

The pilots came and started it up and drove it to the runway. On takeoff, I noticed the steering must be loose and hoped it was the wheel linkage and not the rudder linkage.

132

But after a pleasant two hours flight, in which we were served candy, we wobbled through the air to the runway! After landing, there were a smiling driver, interpreter, and social worker, Mikael, Youry, and Zena, all from Oleg's network, waiting for us with a large Russian vehicle.

We had been told we would stay at a hotel and have to go out for needed interviews and to see the children. I asked if we were on our way to a motel. Youry sort of stammered out, "Well, uh, if it's all right, uh, you are expected at the orphanage. The children are waiting up for you. And they are expecting you to stay there if it's all right." We were nonplused. Twenty-five solid hours of flights, business, traffic, and immigration with no bed or bath, and now this at 9 p.m.! According to the original plans we were to overnight on the train and meet the children in the morning, but they had changed all that! We had been told that Americans smell different in addition to sounding and looking different. I felt sorry for the poor children. What would they think of their fate? We really were excited about it though. So we freshened up and chewed gum to help with the first impressions.

Ulianovsk is a city of one million people. It lies on both sides of the Volga River. Only four furnaces provide heat for the entire city, both heat and hot water. This city, previously named Simbursk, was renamed after Lenin Ulianov, and is still steeped in the old ways of communism and atheism.

The orphanage had around 300 toddlers in a main building. There were outlying duplexes where older children lived. Our three were in one side of such a duplex. Houses in Ulianovsk have an outside door to an inside hall where winter clothes are stored in drawers and closets. The hall leads to the living area and stair. There are a kitchen, laundry, bath, bed, living, and dining rooms on the first floor. Upstairs there is a hall with two girls' rooms and two boys' rooms. At the end of the hall are two small doors. The one opens to a commode and the other to a sink and bathtub. There were always two caretakers around. The bedrooms had nice bunk beds and a desk. We found the place well kept and clean.

We went into the hall and caught a glimpse of the children we already knew by photos, sitting on the couch in the living room. What must they be wondering? How were they feeling? All I knew was this was exciting and scary.

We took just a little time to take off our coats and then went in. But what to say? Just pat each head and give a hug with, "Hello, Marina! Hello, Natalia! Hi, Ruslin!" etc. And remember to say the Russian pronunciation. (We soon found out Natalia was commonly called Natasha in Russia. We struck out on that one.) Then we held them and jabbered English and whatever Russian we knew and took pictures. All the English they knew was "Mama," "Papa," and "I love you." Later they made sentences like, "Mama, I love you. Papa, I love you." The words for parents are the same in Russia and they had a little bear that said, "I love you," when you squeezed its paw.

Then it was off to bed for them, and supper, bath, and bed for us. Our room had two single beds 24″ wide.

The next day we ate too much because we didn't realize the one table session was supposed to be morning tea. At noon, true to custom, our dinner was served to us in plates already filled. There was a large bowl of chicken noodle soup each, and a large well-filled plate with mashed potatoes and half a chicken each. We could hardly eat it because we were still full from our breakfast omelets and morning tea. But we also felt we must eat it since they were so generous and this was so far above what the children got.

That day was full. We had meetings with the doctor and officials from the Ministry of Education (social services).

Zena, especially, became a faithful friend and advocate, and a friend to the children. At one point we noticed Marina speaking to her. Later we found out she was saying, "I want them to be my mom and dad." We signed a number of papers, waiving a waiting period, saying we actually wanted the children. Then it was time for the children's naps, so we helped them to bed. I can still see a little girl sitting up in bed, leaning to wave as we walked by in the hall.

After paying our dues quite quickly, we were off to the train for the 16 hours back to Moscow. When the children awoke they would find us gone. We often wondered how that made them feel. Later Marina said they were disappointed. It would be three months almost to the day before we could come back. We had expected four or five weeks.

After 16 hours on the train we arrived in Moscow. As we gathered our luggage we wondered how we would find anyone we knew in the crowd. Now that could be scary. What a blessing to see Stepon's friendly face, looking in the train window just as we were about ready to open our private compartment door.

More Homework. *Paperwork We Had to Do Upon Return:*

1. *Petition to Adjudicate Adoption of Children, notarized and apostilled.*
2. *Medical documents had to be changed to current date, notarized, and apostilled.*
3. *I-171H had to be apostilled.*
4. *We had to prepare, notarize, and apostille Power of Attorney for Fern.*
5. *My employment letter had to be rewritten, notarized, and apostilled.*
6. *Criminal background record check had to be updated, notarized, and apostilled.*

We returned from Russia on Friday, the 9th of November. That same night we made announcements with pictures, complete with names and ages. It was past midnight when we got done, and we misspelled words!

Since we were to leave for our son Jimmie's wedding in Missouri the following Tuesday, the 13th, we had to move fast on the paperwork. We couldn't get the medical documents done, so sent off numbers 1, 3, 4.

We were back in Virginia again the 20th, Tuesday p.m. Wednesday we tried for the medical documents again. Between then and Thanksgiving we got Village Medical to fix the papers, but they had the date wrong. And now they wouldn't look at the papers anymore. Ann from ABC Adoption Services said get the tests and go to another doctor. But our doctor's receptionist finally said they would do them. They were closed from Thanksgiving through Friday, Saturday, and Sunday. So Monday we went in, expecting to take the finished papers from there to the office of the Sec. of The Commonwealth. But they again would not cooperate and told us to leave the papers. I knew they would be filled in incorrectly again so I requested an appointment. "You don't need to see the doctor," they said. So the next day we left Johnny at Dad's so he could take him to school, and we went in early, without an appointment for a walk-in doctor visit. We finally got to see a doctor and the thing was fixed.

Then the new judge in Russia kicked out #5 because I needed a job and salary instead of being partner and getting a salary range. Also #6 had been done in July and the judge said it needed to be dated more recently. So we rushed them off.

We had a great time shopping for clothes and stuff for the children. Layers of clothing, several sets each. Then a crib, car seats, seat belts, toys, etc.

That was hurry, hurry! Then we waited and waited.

The Call Comes. Christmas came and slowed the American ability to process and send papers. In January the Russians had Christmas. Then there were personnel changes or new rulings in Moscow. It was like waiting for the

Lord's return, expecting a call every day and not getting one.

1/23/02-I was going to call Ann yesterday, but she was busy. I got the confirmation last night by E-mail that the embassy in Moscow had our papers ready. Then today Arlene and I had a good excuse to call Ann and tell her. I tried several times, but she was busy. Then she called about 3:30 p.m. and lo and behold we have a court date, Valentine's Day! We are to leave the 6th and return around the 20th. Dates might change. Now it's hurry, hurry again. We weren't quite as prepared as we thought, maybe. Get tickets, visas, pack, leave directions and itinerary, make arrangements for Johnny, etc.

Also, suddenly we needed medical documents for Johnny. There was no way to get them to Russia in three days, hardly enough time to get them done, period. Somehow we got them done and stamped in time to take them along with us.

The Second Trip. This time we had so much to take along. There were clothes for three children—underwear, dresses, pants, sweaters, scarves, coats, snow pants, knitted caps, gloves. We took lots of clothes for the orphanage too. We had visited Grace Press in Pennsylvania to get Bibles and children's coloring and reading books to give out over there.

Many gifts were taken also. Each person who helped us got something. Officials that we met, and some we didn't meet, our drivers, our interpreters, Mr. Oleg, all were on the list. The gifts included wood carvings locally made in our area with Virginia quarters, books, or chocolate sets. The wines and cigarettes that were suggested didn't suit us.

At the orphanage we gave each helper a good book and perfume set besides tipping them. We felt indebted to them. The older orphan girls got socks or sweaters.

Second Moscow Experience. We were so impressed with Oleg's system of drivers and interpreters that we barely had a worry as we, loaded with money, approached Moscow this time. But when we got through immigration, there was no Sergi to greet us. We moved on into the public area. I told Arlene not to look lost. I didn't want just any old fellow offering us a ride! Soon a bewhiskered man we had never seen before approached us and, in very poor English, told us to come with him. I groped for questions to ask him so we could determine if this man was genuine. I asked, "Who do you work for?" He told me it was Sergi. I drew a blank. I thought he should say Oleg. Any good thug could do that much homework. "What is your name?" He gave his name but I never heard that name before. "Do you have an ID?" He looked blank then smilingly dug out his driver's license. But of course he would have a license if he had a car.

I walked over to a police officer and said I needed help. He motioned that he couldn't talk. But a taxi driver heard me and I told him I needed a phone. "Come on to my office," he said. "Anything you want, I will do." I called Oleg and he assured me that according to my description this was the right man. He would call him on his cell phone. When I got back to Arlene and the luggage, Arlene was talking on the stranger's phone to Oleg. She handed the phone to me and we had our proof.

Their mistake was that they thought he had driven us to the airport in November, but it had been his wife, Julia (the older), an interpreter with a taxi driver. Later I would walk up to him and touch his elbow and ask for an ID. We always got the grins.

After touring Red Square, the Kremlin, and the underground train system, we boarded a train sleeper for our 16-hour trip to Ulianovsk. The country was wrapped in snow and it was cold. The Volga River was frozen three feet deep and dotted with fishermen. We were dressed very well for this cold and were glad for all the layers we brought for the children.

138

Our Reception at the Orphanage. Upon arrival at the orphanage, we stepped into the entrance hall of the duplex. The hall was full of grown-ups from our entourage and orphanage personnel and unrecognized Russian speech was everywhere. Suddenly I became aware of Ruslin's loud voice, "Papa, Papa, Papa!" Dodging grown-up legs he found me, and he jumped up in my arms, giving me hugs and kisses. Just that soon he was scrambling down screaming, "Mama, Mama, Mama!" and was in her arms while Natalia's voice announced her coming in a similar way. But where was eight-year-old Marina? She was standing shyly in the hall waiting for us.

The First Week. We had the same upstairs bedroom, which became home base for the children. Ruslin's crib was moved in with us. The girls slept in with the other orphanage girls.

We were responsible for our children from the start of our one-week stay here. We ate with them, took them on walks, bathed them, and tried hard to control them. They were super-geared-up and excited.

And we didn't know the rules. The interpreter was gone most of the time and we couldn't communicate too well with the caretakers. We wanted to maintain the rules already in place. But was jumping on the top bunk permissible? The only time the caretakers would interfere was when there was excessive crying or we asked them. I think the children got on some nerves besides ours during the first several days until we finally found some ways to control them. The first three days were the worst. One letter home had me saying that out of us five there will be only three survivors, and Arlene and I won't be one of them. Then I thought that maybe there will be no survivors. They will self-destruct.

My feeling at one time was that I have compromised all of my child training ideals. But I reassured myself that it was just for a short time. Rome wasn't conquered in a day.

139

There was fighting and generally upset behavior. We found that making them sit until decibels came to an acceptable level worked. But when the one that was hit last was okayed to go, the first thing on the agenda was to whack the one who hit them last. After several forced sessions we could say, "You want to sit in the chair?" and they usually didn't have to.

The first night we tried to get three-year-old Ruslin to sleep. But he had other plans. He'd toss and turn and sit up. Our options were very limited. I let him rub my arm. I sang to him, which interested him greatly. But nothing worked for long. I used Russian words for "good night," and "quiet" while his wails got louder and louder and more insistent. Finally, one of the girls came from her room and said, "toliet." That was close enough to English that I understood. Can you imagine the poor boy saying, "I got to go to the bathroom!" while this funny new dad was saying, "Quiet, good night, Daddy's here, shhhh"? We soon learned the three words they used for restroom visits.

The next night was worse. There I was for two hours trying to soothe and calm him. Finally I manhandled him onto his side saying, "Spakoynee!" (Quiet). His wails reached high-water mark fast. The caretaker came stumping in and in response to something Ruslin wailed, jerked his pajamas down and checked his leg where I had grabbed him. Seeing nothing, we sensed her dismissing any problem. She talked straight to Ruslin and he settled down . . . for a while. (We later found out they would tell the children that if they made too much noise their new mom and dad would not want them.) Then it would happen all over again. And he would use the magic word, *toliet*. But he didn't have to go. It was just an escape.

So there were two very tired adults. We got to bed last, but the next morning the children were up knocking on our door before we were rested up. And things got out of hand. So we tried getting up and dressed early, getting the children up, and whispering to them. They whispered back and the day went much better with lower decibels.

Each morning after breakfast we would hear, "Papa, goolots, pazshalista?" (Papa, go out, please?) We would all bundle up and take a walk. A light snow had fallen overnight and some of the boys were scraping the road with plywood squares while others shoveled it up on the ridge beside the road. The courtyard had 2′ of snow with paths on top.

Soon most wanted to go back in. Marina wanted a little time with her new dad so we stayed out and learned language on a longer walk.

Inside the orphanage, our bedroom became home base to the children. They would play in the halls and come back in every little bit to administer hugs and kisses, then off again. The children liked their backpacks with their treasures inside. We had coloring, picture and sticker books, dolls, and matchbox toys. We often played with the children.

After the other children ate, it was our turn. We sat together as a family and prayed and ate. Sometimes a video was on and Marina wanted to see it. As vexing as this was, we knew we were in a transition and not all was perfect. They came to us for all their needs. Things were going better.

The Court Trial. There were many sessions with social workers, doctors, etc. We were schooled in answering questions that we would face in court. Methods of punishment were discussed and we were directed to say we didn't use any corporal punishment. Also our farm operation was questioned. The lady from the Ministry of Education asked how many chickens we raised. I told her 80,000, which she could not comprehend. Then she asked how many would fit in

141

this room. Zena and Youry were so cross at her for asking such unnecessary questions. Sometimes Youry would spit in disgust.

An acquaintance had told us that they were asked to lie about having seen their child before they went to see a certain official. There were pretty high consequences if they wouldn't lie. But prayer was answered and God worked it all out. We were assured that in our case all was well and above the law, no worries.

Lo and behold, on the way to the court on Thursday we were told that we were not supposed to have seen pictures or medical documents until we got to Russia, and that we must tell the judge that. We must lie after all. But we prayed.

The court opened with the judge asking us to indicate that we would tell the truth. She sat behind a high counter. We sat facing her. We were not to cross our legs, or even have one foot over the other. To our right were two ladies from the Ministry of Education (social services). They were our advocates. Then there was a lady behind a desk who was to defend the children. To our left was Youry, the interpreter. And finishing off the group was another lady behind her desk to our left who was the court recorder.

As the court session progressed, we could see the lady judge was highly suspicious of us. She told me to explain why we chose Russia, how we chose these children, etc. I told a condensed version of our story. Included in the story I mentioned how, through the agency, we received a letter of invitation to Russia. We came in November and saw the children. At that time we met with the doctor who explained all their physicals. And it was there we signed the papers accepting the children. This, I believe, kept her from specifically asking if we had seen pictures or medical documents before.

There were quite a few questions concerning our religious

beliefs, school, restrictions on the children, etc. Once she asked me, "Do you beat your children?"

I said, "I cannot in anger beat my child." She continued to ask the same question two more times.

The last time I said, "My religion forbids me to respond in anger and beat my child." This seemed to satisfy her.

The one social worker stood and testified about the Mennonites. She read from a book. At first I thought, "What is she finding in a Russian book about the Mennonites?" But there was no worry. She was our advocate!

Arlene was asked about her head covering, who was the most important in her life, and who was the most important in the community. She could witness that way. The answer to the last two questions was, "My husband."

Finally the judge seemed to be smiling more and our people were giving the thumbs up during break.

I was to give the final summing up and petitions. I mentioned that it was a privilege to speak in this court in Ulianovsk, Russia, and that if the court sees fit to grant us the children, we can relate well to their birth country because we have made friends here. "We request the court to waive the ten-day waiting period [gave reasons], and that their names be changed as follows: That Urdin Ruslan Masudovich, born on January 25, 1999, be changed to Ruslin Joseph Mast; and that Urdina Natalia Victorovna, born on October 7, 1997, be changed to Natalia Arlene Mast; and that Urdina Marina Victorovna, born on December 13, 1993, be changed to Marina Jolene Mast; and that the birth dates and birth places remain the same; and that we be named as their parents on their birth certificates."

After a break, the judge came back in and read regulation after regulation, referring to the parts of our case on each one that satisfied the regulation. When she was finished, she read each of the "petitions made to this court." After each she said, "Granted."

The children were ours!! What a special Valentine's Day!!

We don't know quite what the children thought that evening, but I think they could sense a milestone was crossed.

The Trip Back to Moscow. Friday was spent driving here and there placing signatures on many papers. Then we headed for the airline ticket office. It was quite something to see a ticket for Ruslin Joseph Mast instead of Urdin Ruslan Masudovich.

We were so glad for the time we spent with the children at the orphanage before we were on our own with them on any trip. And here we were early Saturday at the airport. The children wandered about a little, but did well. Through the interpreter, we asked a Russian lady to assist us a bit if we needed it. She was traveling on the plane also. When it was time, we all went through the glass doors and walked, slipped, and slid to the plane. The children with their back-packs were strung out ahead of us, latched onto anyone who lent a hand while I helped Arlene keep upright and carry our luggage.

The flight went well. We landed on an icy runway. The pilot used the engines to slow us until we were completely stopped.

This was Moscow, and there was that friendly Stepon again. Ruslin loved to ride on my luggage and that kept him near. The others responded to our wishes quite well.

The Stay at the Hotel. Here we stayed at the Opnehok Hotel for four days. Living together outside the orphanage while we waited for still more paperwork was a good experience in preparation for our trip home. This allowed us to get adjusted and take more control.

It was always hot in the hotel. One side of our window

144

was like a door about 18″ wide. But there were no screens or bars. And we were 19 stories up! So we would entertain the children in another room while the window was open. But even then the air seemed to go out instead of cold air coming in.

When we walked the hall we had to be very careful. We had to hold the hands of Ruslin and Natalia, three and four, or they would dart away. If they got ahead, I had to run past them and get between them and the end of the hall. Because at the end of the hall was the fire escape, and somebody else was hot too. The floor-level, wide-window door was wide open. The fire escape stairway had hardly any banisters! A child could easily fall out!

The ground floor was a large gambling den with food, drink, and other morally depraved options all around. So we learned how to order food to our room. On the first trip we gleefully ordered pizza. But we tossed the meat away and ate what was left. This time I ordered what I thought would be good. Not only did we have to satisfy two adults, but also three finicky children. Thirty dollars' worth of food arrived and still was less than great. Next time Arlene ordered and we had a real feast. Soup. We all liked it.

The most memorable supper was our last in Moscow. Stuffed peppers, rice, stir fry, French fries, bread, and salad. We sat around a coffee table and had a nice orderly meal with a minimum amount spilled and children staying seated most of the time.

The last night of our stay brought the doctor. Each child had a physical exam. Ruslin had fun using the doctor's stethoscope and knee hammer.

That night also we received an itemized record of our in-country expenses from Oleg himself. There was a final financial settling up and instructions for departure in the morning.

The Trip Home. We were early to the international airport in Moscow. The eleven-hour flight home that had appeared impossible before, now seemed within uneasy reach. We were told that Russian women would be glad to help. Also the stewardesses would know both languages. You will have to realize that we still were very limited in our child-control options. The children knew no English, we knew only a few Russian words, and there was no depth to our authority at this time. We kept the children under control quite well in the privacy of the hotel, but public reprimands by Americans to adoptive Russian children would be observed with displeasure by Russians.

I tried to arrange our seating in the plane to give us the most control. That plan was compromised immediately in the confusion of getting everyone settled and the luggage stowed. But it was of God. Marina ended up by the window where she was shielded from the rotten TV by the seats ahead. I was next and Ruslin was by the aisle. Arlene and Natalia occupied two of the seats in the center cluster. I prayed much that the children would be spared from that awful TV. And sure enough, each time Marina had to get up, the TV had some harmless still pictures. It happened every time. I will not mention what was on between times.

We were able to keep the children satisfied and under control the first seven hours fairly well. The children colored, played, and looked at books. But there was no reference point of sitting still and letting the stewardesses serve us and later take the trash. Also we beat a pretty good path to the toilets. And there was always this feeling that this wouldn't last.

Sure enough, Ruslin started to absolutely refuse to be fastened in with a seat belt. The screams were as loud as he could muster. He wanted to run. Yet he loved his new dad. His behavior got so bad that I finally took him to four waiting Russian ladies. The other children soon followed and somewhat settled down. But soon Ruslin was back for a moment on my lap. Then back to them, then up and down the aisles and generally unruly. Natalia, too, was in the other aisle, up ahead with total strangers. I told the lady that I gave the children into her care and expected them to stay with her, and why were they all over the airplane. She tapped my arm and said, "Sir, I took your son, but he said he wanted to go sit on Papa's lap, so I let him go." I saw that he was wrapping her around his finger too.

When we were about to land, we tried to get Ruslin strapped in. Sirens! It got so bad that the stewardess and the lady were kneeling in the aisle trying to calm him. No good. Finally the lady was allowed to hold him while we landed.

When we boarded the short flight from the Kennedy airport to Dulles near Washington, I looked around and figured I was quite happily on my own. The strap went on, the siren hit high, and the legs flew. I said, "Young man, this is where you stay!" and the strap got tighter. A book was offered and hit the floor. A pillow was placed by the little head, and soon I noticed the high notes were flatted a little. It wasn't long until little Ruslin was fast asleep!

It was so nice to see the many members of our family meeting us at the airport. Johnny came to us. He had missed us badly and was just now starting on a new adjustment trip. We were so involved with just us five. But now it was time to be parents to Johnny again.

The car seat was very little problem for the children. They were getting more used to us all the time. And they weren't surrounded with milling people and loud unfamiliar noises.

We stopped for supper at a Cracker Barrel restaurant. The children ate very little. The extended family helped entertain them and they seemed more settled already.

The First Few Days. It was late when we got home. Soon

147

the wide-eyed children were on their way to their new beds. We sang the now familiar songs that we sang in Russia, and they still had their beloved backpacks with familiar treasures.

We were not sure how our curtains, flowers, and furniture would look by the end of the next day. But when the children got up, they were calm and cooperative. This was home! They had Mom and Dad. They were secure.

Communication in the Home. Communication didn't seem to be a problem, mostly. There were times, however, when a child would be frustrated, and we couldn't find common ground. We were a functioning family that used Russian and English words along with gestures. Soon we progressed to English phrases and gestures, and then to simple sentences. At six weeks the children were at a turning point in language. They understood quite a lot of English but spoke little. Soon more and more English words came.

Any new experience brought its language difficulties. Imagine the challenge of explaining a dead deer hit by a car. There was so little vocabulary on either side for that. We used *machina* (car) and *Bambi* (deer from a picture book) with a lot of gestures. The question came, "Doctor?" Now we had to explain *dead* instead of *sick*.

We used the Russian words for *yes* and *no*. But sometimes an answer was "maybe." I held up three fingers and showed one finger for "yes," another for "no," and the center one for "maybe so." "Maybe so" became an oft-used expression.

We recall the first time the girls were talking English to each other in their bedroom. (We had a room monitor.) Also the first time there were arguments in English. Language was coming right along!

We changed some of our meal routines to better fit the children's needs. We usually sing a song and recite a verse, then often use a memorized prayer such as "God Is Great," or the Lord's Prayer. At night we taught them a bedtime prayer, with sometimes an added special request. It amazed us how quickly they learned those words before they knew the meaning.

And we feel the bedtime singing and story times are very important. Putting Ruslin to bed, Dad would sing five songs, then go tuck the girls in and sometimes sing five songs to each girl. Mom had sung her ten songs for the girls already and was down with Ruslin singing five more. They were very good at keeping track who had how many songs.

Later, with difficulty, we reduced this to one song each and, when they started to understand, a story. They especially like stories about our trip to Russia and about them.

Of course, at first books were used for pictures only. I still remember someone making a remark to the children about Jonah. I told the person that they never heard about Jonah. It was later that Bible stories could be told and they were relished. It was truly incredible how quickly they learned.

A Year Later. By consistent discipline and teaching, our meals are quieter now and quite conversational. We always required at least a taste of the most despicable foods. Peas, beans, and corn can now be enjoyed without vomiting. Actually, there are no foods that cause any unusual problems.

Marina had to catch up in phonics, sounding out words she never heard before. Her reading is improving so much that she is on the verge of becoming a bookworm. Natalia won't go to school next year, but can recognize some numbers. Ruslin can take a catalog and find tools just like Dad's, and others he thinks Dad might need.

Was there ever a time without our children? Yes, a long, long time ago. So much has been crammed into so short a time that it seems like years. But in reality, we applied with Carolina Adoption Services in May 2001. In November we took our first trip. February 20, 2002, we were back home with the children.

God has certainly blessed us with a happy, obedient, loving family. We want to bring them up to trust and obey Him.

14

Norman & Karen Mast

Daryl Lynn — *May 19, 1998*

Jo Etta Fern — *October 7, 2000*

Anthony Homer — *August 11, 2002*

—Goshen, Indiana

When we married in 1991, we naturally dreamed of having children. When year after year passed, we decided to see a doctor. What a shock to discover God wouldn't bless us with biological children. Oh, how could we live without children in our lives? We loved children. Time passed and we felt God telling us adoption might be our answer.

We decided to talk with our neighbors, Thomas and Rhoda Bontrager. After our second visit with them, we knew adoption was for us. They answered questions, gave advice, and lots of encouragement. After checking with doctors' offices and the Goshen Hospital for leads and finding none, we started our home study and signed up with Silver Spoon Adoptions in January 1998. Four months later on May 19, little Daryl Lynn was born in Idaho.

The next morning my parents and Karen's brother and sister went with us on the Greyhound. We arrived in Idaho May 22nd in late evening. The next day we got our first little blessing from God. Oh, how happy we were! We actually are a mom and daddy now! We were blessed with a healthy baby!

We felt we were ready to start for a second one January 2000. We contracted with Heart of Gold. It sounded so promising! We were matched with a birthmother from Alabama. On July 4, 2000, she had a baby girl. So both our parents went with us. This was a closed adoption, so we were in contact only with the lawyer in Alabama. We went to the hospital and held the baby. She wasn't released from the hospital yet, so we went to the hotel. The social worker met us there. She said the birthmother wants an open adoption after all. When she found out we are Amish, she said she didn't want us for the baby's parents. She didn't know anything about Amish, and she wasn't interested in finding out either. We thought maybe if she met us, she might change her mind, but she didn't want to meet us. What could we do except go home empty-handed. Oh, so hard!!! Why, Lord? We didn't have the answer, but we knew there was a reason. God had other plans for us. Two months later Silver Spoon contacted us and said they have a birthmother in Ohio, due in October.

We had a conference call with the birthmother and birthfather. They were excited and said, "We're matched." On October 7, 2000, baby Jo Etta Fern was born. Oh, what joy!! It was on my birthday! Was it too good to be true?

We had a public auction to sell our house on October 10, so we had to wait until the sale was past. Then my parents took another trip with us to get our bundle of joy! Jo Etta was being fussy when we got to the hospital, but when we held her, she settled down and slept for hours. The next day we brought her home. Our family was growing, and we were so happy.

In January 2002, we talked with the owner of Heart of Gold. Since our contract was about to expire, we thought we might be able to work out something. He said he'd tell everyone that we're on the list again. February, March, April, still we heard nothing. In May our contract was to expire, but he said for more money, he'd extend it. We contacted Jennifer again to see about going with her once more. "Oh, Lord, we pray, what is Your will? Which route are we to take? Are we making the right decisions? We want to do what's best."

It seemed the answer was to go with Jennifer at Silver Spoon, and drop Heart of Gold for the present time. In July 2002, Jennifer contacted us and said she had a birthmother in Arizona. We talked with the birthmother, and she was excited about an Amish family. She wanted me to keep in contact with her, so I called her repeatedly. We bonded very quickly. On August 11, 2002, Anthony Homer was born. A couple hours later, we were packed and ready to get on the Amtrak. My parents (Karen's) and youngest brother went with us. We again needed their support, which we were thankful for beyond words! We got baby Anthony on our eleventh anniversary. We met the birthmother. It is something we will never forget.

It was heartbreaking to see how much she loved him and wanted him. It was very hard for her to see her baby boy for the last time. Oh, how our hearts ached for her. I can't put into words what we witnessed!

On August 17th we were home with our third miracle baby. God has blessed us with so much. Three healthy children, and life is so much more fulfilling. The birthmothers are a part of us and are very close in our hearts. What would life be without them? Our families, friends, and community have been very supportive of us. We can't explain how much this means to us.

We never had any contact with Daryl's birthmother. She placed a girl for adoption, a year before Daryl was born, with contact, and felt she wasn't able to handle having contact again.

We communicated with Jo Etta's birthmother through

letters and occasional phone calls, then over last Christmas we had the privilege of meeting her. It was a wonderful experience, something we can't explain!

For Anthony's birthmother we had a lot of phone contact. We met her at birth. Again, something we can't explain—to see her pain, and our gain! It almost didn't seem fair to take her baby.

All of our birthmothers are very dear to us!

We would encourage anyone who is childless to give adoption a consideration. We cannot imagine life without our children. Being married seven years before our first miracle, cannot be compared to life with a family. We are thankful that God opened the doors for adoption. Our children definitely were born for us.

"May God bless you like He has blessed us."

Different Trips to the Same Place

(Adoption Allegory)

Deciding to have a baby is like planning a trip to Australia. You've heard it's a wonderful place, you've read many guidebooks, and feel certain you're ready to go. Everybody you know has traveled there by plane. They say it can be a turbulent flight with occasional rough landings, but you can look forward to being pampered on the trip.

So you go the airport and ask the ticket agent for a ticket to Australia. All around you, excited people are boarding planes for Australia. It seems there is no seat for you; you'll have to wait for the next flight. Impatient, but anticipating a wonderful trip, you wait—and wait—and wait.

Flights to Australia continue to come and go. People say silly things like, "Relax. You'll get on a flight soon." Other people actually get on a plane and then cancel their trip, to which you cry, "It's not fair!"

After a long time the ticket agent tells you, "I'm sorry, we're not going to be able to get you on a plane to Australia. Perhaps you should think about going by boat."

"By BOAT!" you say. "Going by boat will take a very long time and it costs a great deal of money. I really had my heart set on going by plane." So you go home and think about not going to Australia at all. You wonder if Australia will be as beautiful if you approach it by sea rather than air. But you have long dreamed of this wonderful place, and finally you decide to travel by boat.

It is a long trip, many months over many rough seas. No one pampers you. You wonder if you will ever see Australia. Meanwhile, your friends have flown back and forth to Australia two or three more times, marveling about each trip.

Then one glorious day, the boat docks in Australia. It is more exquisite than you ever imagined, and the beauty is magnified by your long days at sea. You have made many wonderful friends during your voyage, and you find yourself comparing stories with others who also traveled by sea rather than by air.

People continue to fly to Australia as often as they like, but you are able to travel only once, perhaps twice. Some say things like, "Oh, be glad you didn't fly. My flight was horrible; traveling by sea is so easy."

You will always wonder what it would have been like to fly to Australia. Still, you know God blessed you with a special appreciation of Australia, and the beauty of Australia is not in the way you get there, but in the place itself.

—Author Unknown

156

15

Willis & Esther Schwartz

Matthew Alan — *June 4, 2000*

—Burnsville, North Carolina

We were married on June 8, 1989, in LaGrange, Indiana. The first five years of our marriage we lived in Adam County, Indiana. In October of 1994 we moved to LaGrange, Indiana. I taught school and enjoyed working with the children. But I always had this longing to have a child of our own. In January of 1998 we had some counseling from the ministers, and they encouraged us to check into adoption. We talked it over with our parents, and they supported us and encouraged us.

We checked out different options. We got in contact with Norman and Karen Mast, who had signed up with Silver Spoon Adoptions. We got some more information from them and decided to go with Silver Spoon Adoptions too. We signed up in May of 1998. Now came the waiting part.

Silver Spoon Adoptions called us in August 1998 about a baby that was to be born in October. We were very excited and didn't realize the ups and downs we were yet to face. The first of October we were told that this baby was going to be placed with family. It was hard to accept at first, but now we can see that God was testing our faith, and showing us that this was not the child He wanted us to have.

In the spring of 1999 we were contacted about a baby girl that was to be born in June. We had contact with the birth-mom. We shared family history and other concerns she had.

She wanted us to be there when her baby was born. This birthmom was living in California. We had contacted an attorney from her area to work with her. On June 7, 1999, my parents, Willis' parents, and we left for California. We did some sightseeing on the way out. We were on our way to meet her when the attorney called and said she decided to keep her baby. We were 2,000 miles from home and very discouraged.

We went back home and tried to go on with life. The church and friends were very supportive and encouraged us to go on. I was ready to give up. We had more possibilities come up, but it seemed they just weren't right for us. Our

Willis Schwartz family

contract with Silver Spoon Adoptions ran out in May of 2000, and we were still without a child.

In May of 2000 we were contacted about a little boy that was to be born in June. The birthmom was staying in Utah at this time. We were scared to get our hopes up. They told us that they scheduled a C-section for June 9, 2000, and would like for us to be there. So we made reservations to travel via Amtrak. We had our tickets to leave on June 7, 2000. On Sunday, June 4, 2000, we had gone to the neighbors for the day. When we got home we had a message that our little boy was born at 12:03 a.m. on June 4, 2000. What a day! To know that a baby is waiting in Utah for us to come and pick up—our very own son. Needless to say we did some fast rearranging and left from Chicago on the Amtrak at 3 p.m. on Monday, June 5, 2000. We arrived in Provo, Utah, at 11:30 p.m. on June 6, 2000. Julie (a worker from the agency there) picked us up and took us to our motel.

There was no sleep in sight for me that night as we had found out that the birthmom was caring for the baby at the hospital, and that she had not signed any papers yet. The question was, Did we come all this way again for another disappointment? Julie had told us she seems very committed as she didn't have much to offer him and wanted a two-parent home for him. She was a single girl 34 years old.

On June 7, 2000 (one day before our eleventh anniversary), we met the birthmom at the agency and a tiny 6 lb. baby boy was placed in our arms by the birthmom. We cried and shared some family history together while admiring this special little boy. She had named him Evan Lee, but seemed happy with the name of Matthew Alan that we had chosen for him. It was a very touching experience, but oh, so special. She asked that we take good care of her little boy.

We spent nine days at the motel in Provo bonding and enjoying our bundle of joy. But we were anxious to go home to share him with family and friends. Everybody accepted him just like any other baby. Matthew was always scared of men, and my dad was no exception. It was hard on Dad that he was not allowed to hold him. He seemed extra special to my dad.

In July of 2001 we moved to Quaker City, Ohio, and lived there for a year and then moved to Burnsville, North Carolina. We attend Sprucepine Believers Fellowship. Willis is a carpenter and builds houses. Matthew has brought many happy and memorable moments into our lives. He has always been a healthy child.

In August of 2001 Matthew's birthmom spent two nights in our home. It was a good experience for us. She told us after seeing that Matthew is happy and cared for that she made the right choice. We have been blessed with having Matthew in our home and are waiting for the opportunity to adopt another child.

Adopted . . .

by Mary June Glick

You are adopted—
   the circumstances of your life
   may be different from many people,
   but that doesn't make you different!
   You experienced separation from the parents
   who gave you birth.
God provided a family for you—
   a family who loves and cares,
   just as if you had been born to them.
God plans for you to enjoy life—
   to love those who love you.
   Even though you may wonder
   about your birth family,
   that's okay, that's normal.
Accept your situation in life—
   and use it to be sensitive to others.
   Everyone has some pain, some hurt,
   to cope with, even if
   he is not adopted!
   Reach out and allow God to use
   your unique experiences to touch others!
God used many great men and women—
   in the Bible, who were adopted,
   or grew up in a home
   away from their birth parents.

Moses, adopted by the king's daughter—
    lived in a palace. Yet God used
    him to lead the children of Israel
    out of Egypt, into the promised land!
Samuel, whose mother brought him to the temple—
    at an early age,
    could have felt rejection, but he
    listened and obeyed God!
Esther, was raised by her uncle—
    and she became a queen,
    who saved her people!
The little maid—
    who told Captain Naaman about Elisha,
    saved her master
    from the dreaded disease of leprosy!
Even Jesus—
    left His Father's house.
    God provided an earthly family for Him,
    but He often experienced rejection;
    yet He ministered to people.
    He felt their hurts, their pain,
    and He loved them!
God's purposes—
    may seem hard to understand,
    but rest assured,
    He does have a purpose and a plan
    for your life.
    He may just desire to use you
    in a very special way,
Because you are adopted!

16

Carl & Noreen Sensenig

Regina — *December 17, 1969*

Sidney Owen — *April 27, 1971*

Stanley Evan — *October 24, 1973*

Ruthana — *February 5, 1975*

Seth John — *November 21, 1975*

Rosalynn — *April 15, 1977*

Joshua Tibor — *September 24, 1979*

Ethan Joel — *February 15, 1981*

Justin Samuel — *June 12, 1984*

Mary Kate — *July 17, 1987*

Meg Kristine — *June 28, 1988*

—Seneca Falls, New York

To some folks the word *adoption* conjures up thoughts of mystery, rescue, or living happily ever after. As a young married couple, living in southern Lancaster County, Pennsylvania, my husband Carl and I were no exception to this. With only a faint idea of the involvement of adoption or foster care, but with a love for children, we inquired as to its possibilities for us.

But first of all, God had other things in mind. He clearly wanted us to sharpen our parenting skills on the five, healthy biological babies He so graciously gave us. We were awed and thrilled with each new one. Thoughts of adding to the quiver-full were diminished with the pressing duties of daily life and the joys and pleasures of little bodies and souls to nurture. In the meantime, Carl was ordained to the ministry with more souls to care for and less time to go around.

However, when our youngest was well over two and our oldest ten years old, we felt a renewed urge to make the difference in the life of just one, even though there are so many sad children who have dysfunctional homes. Carl liked the illustration of the man who was throwing back into the ocean small sea creatures which had accidentally washed onto the beach. "There are so many, why bother," someone asked. Keeping right on, he said, "But this one shall live!"

Local foster care, usually the easiest way to find needy children, opened a door for us. An excited three-year-old was

Carl Sensenig family

brought to an equally excited and thrilled Mennonite family. We had asked for a child that may be relinquished. We thought it a good sign when he walked right over to our four-year-old and put a little hand on each cheek. At that time we were not so much concerned about physical problems a child may bring with him. It seemed God closed our eyes to that, so that S. John could have a home. Our robust bright-eyed boy showed signs of mild autism, a little-understood problem in 1979. Our hearts ached as he walked and walked searching for familiar places and people. The playpen that he was left in previously for long periods of time would have held the comfort of the known and proven. After periods of letting us know his frustration by emptying toothpaste tubes and noncompliance with the expected, he gradually gave us his heart. John continues to bless our home and the church today. He was given an exceptional memory, which aided him in school. He has many Scriptures and songs committed to memory, besides facts about people. He participates in public worship with devotionals and topics.

A few years later we were blessed with our fifth biological child, a son, E. Joel, making seven offspring. At this time too, a privately run home was taking in older children in the Bernville, Pa., area. Reaching their saturation point, they referred children to us, mostly older children whom we would refer to our church's (now established) child-care committee. With all the work possibilities on our hog farm, we would have some of the 14- or 15-year-old boys stay with us. While younger children seem more helpless and needy, older ones, including teens, are no less in need of loving, stable homes where they can see the Gospel lived out. It is probably easiest if there are no other growing children in the home. Watchfulness and constant assessment of the other children can take its toll on parents. Most often, a close-knit family of children can be a wonderful example to the new-comer, and more likely than not, the family may be grossed out by the immature behavior of the newcomer rather than negatively influenced.

An older child has more experience and consciousness of rejection than a younger one does. Therefore an older one may need more reassurance and approval. One girl in foster care said the older she got, the hungrier she was for a loving, stable home, but the angrier and more defensive she felt for being let down. Taking in older children or teens requires much prayer for wisdom.

Adoption lay before us. The Spanish mother from a poor section of the city of Reading seemed adamant about her decision. In telephone contacts we let her know that we were waiting and anticipating with her, and that our hearts were getting involved. "Please don't let us down," we pleaded. March slowly approached, and with a few misgivings we bought a new aqua sweater set.

It was a boy, and yes, she's ready to leave the hospital. She had seen the baby and held it. Would she change her mind? Finally, we were all in the car, Carl and I, new mother and baby. We held our breaths as we approached her city apart-ment. She thanked us for the ride and got out, leaving the little black-haired infant with us!

By now, our six were acquainted with the coming and going of foster children. But, when the call came from the mother that she changed her mind, it was very difficult. Six weeks had lapsed. The baby had started to smile in response to our coaxing, and he was usually in someone's arms. Again, she was firm, this was her child and now he was going home. The arguments from us seemed to fall on deaf ears, and we knew the law was on her side. All we had was the goodwill of the parent. We took him back shortly, to a dark, smoky room, and said tearful good-byes.

166

That was the precursor to our search for a baby we could keep. There were no more Sensenig infants, and it appeared there were no other babies for us period. We checked with every possible agency. Healthy white babies were in high demand. Some could be gotten after years of waiting, and paying the price of a farm! Overseas adoptions were also very expensive. Friends of ours—some childless, were also searching. We felt for them, as they ached for a family. Part of our search was for them as well.

The desire to adopt did not get any less as time went by. We were able to get some pictures from an orphanage in El Salvador—pictures of older children. There were other blind leads, still we felt the "birth" waiting pangs of some little one out there somewhere. Some agencies seemed so heartless, especially when they learned we already had six. All we wanted to do was to help one little baby who didn't have anybody to belong to. We read of needy children, but why couldn't there be connections to loving arms?

Finally, the door was flung wide open. It was 1984, and there was a need for a home for bi-racial infants. In a few weeks, the angel social worker was sitting in our living room saying, "We have this four-month-old, little boy, whose mother is anxious to have him placed." Bethany Christian Services did a wonderful job of starting out our baby Justin in a good foster home, so that he never knew a want or care. Soon he was settled in, on our mountain farm.

Two years later, Bethany Christian Services again heard our pleas for a baby. Friends also heard about this opportunity and were blessed with healthy bi-racial babies, but the door began to close. Soon families were not admitted who did not have higher education goals for their children.

Our girls were very excited. Two of them climbed on top of a small grain bin by the driveway to get a first glimpse at baby Mary Kate. Dolls were laid aside as this precious dusty-brown

167

cherub wound her way into our hearts. We did not need to fear long about a "colored" baby. She and her brother were well accepted. Some of our older relatives who had lived with fears of the black people on the Welsh mountains expressed their concerns. However, these precious ones often with a black father and white mother needed homes, and years later are now among God's friends.

The last part of our adoption journey was the most arduous but most rewarding. We were privileged in 1991, to visit the infamous orphanages in Romania, with four dossiers in our belongings—two for Carl's cousin and family and two for us. With 2½-year-old Mary Kate in tow we tramped in and out of huge warehouses of children. It was incredible! Each sizeable town had three sizes of orphanages. It was heartbreaking, as sick-looking children thronged us. Babies rocked alone in their cribs, even after supper when there should be family time. We prayed much. With a time limit, we asked to see those whose parents lived nearby, as we needed their approval and signatures. We needed to do the legal work ourselves but saved ourselves an enormous fee. God was good to us. The interpreters knew of a newborn. She was baby number one. Baby number two was a slim little three-year-old with a gentle smile. We also started work on "our boy" who stood out above the rest, God having the spotlight on him for us. After fearing he couldn't be released legally, we started proceedings on another boy, who then became afraid of us, hearing that Americans use children for body parts. Suddenly the first boy (now Joshua) was brought in and, with his father's blessing, released to go to the courthouse for an adoption ceremony. The work was very tedious and time-consuming. Everything needed to go through a translator and documents needed to be certified. There were long waits in cold, crowded, smoky hallways.

We also found a lovely blue-eyed, blond eight-year-old girl.

168

Little Edit's father was willing to let her go, but we could not locate the mother. Just as Carl and Mary Kate were ready to leave for home, we heard that the mother is negative to adoption. After three more weeks of strenuous legal work in ancient conditions, I was ready to fly with three children. At the last minute, a new law was filed, which hindered getting their visas. Desperate to get home, I was able to leave the children with godly German-speaking people and a Bucharest friend, and fly home, having been gone six weeks. Our Joshua was put on the plane a week later, and the two little girls for Carl's relative came later.

It was a time of rejoicing, witnessing how miraculously our new eleven-year-old son was led to us. He was a very happy but very sober young lad. He had known much abuse and neglect which he needed to tell us about over and over. This was good. There was so much he had to learn, but it was true, that Joshua didn't really care how much we knew, but first needed to know how much we care.

We probably did not fully realize the impact of the violence and abuse and neglect he had known, and we thought he would soon forget, surrounded by a happy family and kind friends. He gave his heart to the Lord, quite sincerely, at a young age. However, he seemed to be living his past too much, and at age 17, we asked John Beiler in Idaho to help him. After coming back several years later, there was continued sowing of wild oats, and reliving the past. Lately there has been regret for his prodigal ways. Through this time of disappointment, we endeavored to keep an openness, expressing our love and concerns as we had opportunity. This is now paying us well.

Our eleventh and last child, Meg Kristine, was also from Romania. The remaining dossier was "burning a hole in our pocket." With a push from friends who would also go if we did, we reluctantly left our family, but for only a week this time, to find our little girl.

A lawyer did our paperwork for a sizable fee. The third day, he took us to a barn in the country which housed some families. There we found our little Meg. Our childless friends got their little three-year-old son. We wanted a child that direly needed us. At three years, Meg only allowed us to bottle-feed her. Her development and actions were more like a six-month-old baby. She could not sit up well, let alone stand. Meg's favorite pastime was lying on her back, and playing with her bottle. It was a pleasure to watch her rapidly change to age-appropriate activities, now that she at last had a family, instead of busy orphanage personnel.

It was heartwarming to receive congratulatory remarks or cards, even though some folks thought we were going overboard with eleven children. We had many, many inquiries about finding children in Romania and about finding Christian homes in the States. We know it was only because of His Great Guiding Hand.

17

John & Irene Trinier

Benjamin John — *April 27, 1993*

—Manitoba, Canada

After being married sixteen years with no children, our lives have been changed and blessed since Benny came into our home. We have learned it takes much prayer and patience. Example is a very important part of training in a child's life.

We were married April 23, 1977. We looked into adoption in the '80s but nothing materialized. In the fall of 1992, we were told of a young girl interested in making an adoption plan. We prayed about it and made contact with a great aunt that was responsible for the young girl.

Two months before the baby was born, they called to say that we were chosen to be the baby's parents. Of course that was exciting news! We had phone conversations with them. They were friendly and confident that this was the course they wanted to take.

It was early morning, April 27, 1993, when we received the call that the baby was soon to be born. "Could you come right away?"

We had 22-month-old twin foster boys at the time, so my mother consented to take care of them while we made the eleven-hour trip to Goshen, Indiana, for our precious bundle! It seemed like a long drive, arriving at Thomas Bontragers around 10:30 in the evening. Rhoda called the hospital to see if we would be allowed to visit our new son

171

yet that evening. They said that would be fine, so Thomas and Rhoda took us in, and we first met the birthmother, her mother, and our son Benny when he was a little more than nine hours old.

It hardly seemed real! It brought mixed feelings—excitement, and yet also apprehension. The next morning we went to the hospital again, happily taking our diaper bag and baby supplies along. They let me dress Benny, but then

John Trinier family

the birthmother wanted to take him along home for the day.

We still needed to sign papers, and in our minds we wondered if she would still change her mind. That day she took him to school to show him off to her friends! That afternoon we met her in town. She let us have him for several hours as Rhoda was having a baby shower for us. After the shower, we again met her somewhere, and she took him home for the night. That gave us a shaky feeling, but we wanted to cooperate as best we could. The next morning we again met, but this time at the lawyer's office where we both signed papers, and Benny was given to us for keeps at two days old. It is hard to describe the feelings we had!

We started home that day, driving as far as Harrison, Michigan, where we spent the night with friends. Benny was fussy that night, having had experiences two-day-old babies normally don't have! His bed that night was a drawer, as they didn't have a crib.

Benny is our only child and very special to us. We thank the Lord for letting us have a family, though there are only three of us.

We have recently moved from Pelkie, Michigan, to Garland, Manitoba, where we are farming.

We Know the Things of Earth Won't Last

We know the things of earth won't last,
No matter how we try.
They bring us but a fleeting joy
And then they fade and die.

Our investments lie not in our worth,
Our possessions or our gold.
Instead they lie in children—
They're the treasures that we hold.

They bring us even greater joy
Than we ever thought we'd find—
The kind of joy that lasts and lasts—
Not the fleeting kind.

And when we pass those pearly gates
And God's face we finally see,
We know our legacy left behind
Will last eternally.

Written by Mary Jane Proft.
Reprinted with permission of *Mary Sue Originals*.

18

Daniel & Eunice Yoder

Angela Rose — *June 4, 1987*

Anthony Eugene — *July 28, 1988*

Alvin Daniel — *January 28, 1996*

—Leburn, Kentucky

Daniel and I were married in October, 1983. We made our first home in Leburn, Kentucky, where Daniel had lived ever since he was two years old. Life was bright and joy was ours to share. With time, we began to realize our dreams and desires for children seemed evasive. We prayed for a baby. We sought medical help. We longed for something to fill our empty, aching arms, hearts, and home. The doctor told us there was a 10% or less possibility of having biological children. What a blow! What next? "Well, Lord, You have some purpose for our lives; help us find it and fill it for Your honor and glory."

In the spring of '87, four years into married life, our church school in Leburn asked me to teach the lower grades. It was an answer to prayer, something to fill my time and something with children. Daniel worked as a heating and air conditioning technician at the time. During the spring of '88, the Fellowship Mission Board asked us to serve a three-year term in the Dominican Republic, as houseparents for the VS boys, and as mission mechanic. Our prayer still was, "Father, use us as You will and where." So August 31, 1988, found us leaving native soil for the Dominican Republic, a

175

land of the unknown for us. What would these three years hold? God knew!

They held adjustments, a new language, a new culture, a new diet, new brothers and sisters in Christ, and many "firsts." It was a growing experience for us, and God was very near and dear. I taught school for 1¼ years during our time there. Daniel was busy in the shop but still found time to make friends with many of the children at church and in the neighborhood. Still we longed and prayed for children of our own. We visited different children's homes, asking if they had children for adoption. Each time the answer came back, "We just care for these children. They are not up for adoption." We would journey back home, in faith committing it all to God, many times with tear-filled eyes.

Daniel Yoder family

About a year after arriving in the Dominican Republic, we contacted the Social Services in the capitol, asking how we could adopt a baby in the country. They told us we first needed to get residency, and then there would be lots of paperwork, after which they would put us on their list. We could then expect to wait six months to a year for a child. Even though we wanted a baby now, we pursued what they told us, many times praying to our heavenly Father, "Prepare this child for us, and prepare us for this child." Years before we knew it, God was doing just that.

In January of 1991, Daniel called the agency to see if we had been approved yet. "No, not yet. It will be several weeks until the Board meets to review your application. But we will let you know as soon as you are approved."

Two weeks later, on a Thursday afternoon, the telephone rang. It was our social worker. I listened breathlessly, anxiously, as Daniel and the social worker conversed. "Are we approved?" We've waited so long for this! Daniel hung up the receiver, and, turning to me with a smile, said, "They have a boy and a girl for us—an abandoned brother and sister, about 2½ and 3½ years old respectively. They know we asked for a baby, but they do need a home now for these two children. Would we consider?"

Oh, what joy, yet mixed emotions! Should we still wait for a baby, or was God saying, "These are My children I've been preparing for you?" We prayed and prayed some more. We called both sets of parents, seeking their advice. We counseled with families on the mission field. Every light seemed green. Early Monday morning, we left for the capitol 3½ hours away. January 28, 1991—what would it hold? Would we come home with empty arms once more? Or would we be Daddy and Mama?

Our first stop was some business for the mission, then on to the children's home. How well we remember sitting and

177

waiting in the foyer and watching numerous children go by. Which boy and girl might be ours? Soon the social worker and one of the staff came, and called us in, and introduced us to our son- and daughter-to-be. We talked with the children and workers, then, with confidence that God was leading us, we told them we would take Angela Rose and Anthony Eugene (the new names we were giving them) to be our children. Words could scarcely describe our joy! We had asked for one; God gave us two! For these children we prayed, and we will continue to pray for them till our dying day, because they are our children.

We now had the children, but there was still much paperwork to be done. We paid a social worker from the States to come down and do a three-day home study for us while we were still in the Dominican Republic. She came on a Thursday and left the following Tuesday, living with us during that time. For the next nine months we did paperwork between the States and the Dominican Republic. My sister and husband had adopted two children from Honduras just a few months previously and were a tremendous help in securing the necessary documents and in knowing what offices to contact, etc. In October, 1991, we finally obtained the children's visas and flew back to the States. We lived in Pennsylvania for the first six months since our social worker and agency were from there. By March, 1992, all the paperwork was finished and the long awaited day came—the adoption was to be completed. We left the judge's chambers with great joy in our hearts. From the day they had entered our home, we counted them ours. Now they were officially ours! Truly a gift from God!

From the beginning we have freely talked of Anthony and Angela being adopted and how God answered our prayers. How well I remember one day when Anthony was six years old, we were up by the garden burning some trash. He took

178

me by the hand and led me to a seat on a log saying, "Mama, tell me again about the day you got me," with a beaming smile on his face. At times they have shared their longing to see their birthparents, just so they know whom they look like. We share with them that we can understand that longing. If we were in their shoes, we would also want to see whom we looked like. For our children, it will probably never be possible, as they were abandoned and nothing is known of their parents or family.

In the spring of 1992, after the adoption was completed, we returned to the hills of Kentucky, where we still live. In 1994, Daniel was ordained minister for the Valley View Mennonite congregation, here in Leburn, Kentucky. We opened a small bulk food store and later expanded to include a bakery as well, with hopes of working at home with our children as they grew. They are already a real help.

January 28, 1991, is a very special day for us and always will be. January 28, 1996, five years later also became a very special day for us. This was the day Alvin Daniel, our third child, entered our home by birth, after twelve years of married life. The same joy filled our hearts as when Anthony and Angela came into our home. Each child is a gift to cherish, to love, and to guide.

One thing we have been so grateful for is a supportive brotherhood. At school the children all mingle together in work and play. I remember one time when the sisters were gathered for sewing. One grandmother was sitting beside me, and as the schoolchildren came bustling in through the door, she said, "Your son is such a gentleman." Those words were special to me.

That evening, when Anthony said to me, "Mama, I wish I looked like someone, like Alvin does," that grandmother's words came back to me. I replied, "Son, more important than looking like someone else is being someone God can

179

use," and I shared with him those words, "Your son is such a gentleman." He was greatly encouraged by that thoughtful grandmother. Another time an aunt told Angela as she stood by my side, "You have a smile just like your mother." Later she expressed how much that meant to her—she really belonged.

As we look ahead to the future, we wonder what all it will hold for our children. But we are confident that the same God who brought them into our home and lives will continue caring for them on through life. Our prayer is that God would continue to direct us as parents as we in turn endeavor to give direction to these dear souls He has entrusted into our care and who we love so much.

ennis and Clara had been married for six and a half

19

Dennis & Clara Yoder

Maria Joy — *February 19, 2001*
Amanda Grace — *December 24, 2002*
Sandra Hope — *September 5, 2003*

—Goshen, Indiana

D ennis and Clara had been married for six and a half years and the thought of adopting had crossed their minds now and then in the last couple of years. Perhaps it was more so for Clara than for Dennis. After Clara's "false pregnancy," adoption tugged at her heart even more than she or her family realized. Dennis admitted that his selfish nature liked things the way they were. Dennis and Clara both love to read, and Dennis really treasured their early evenings! He is a woodworker by trade and owns his own business, Hoosier House Furnishings.

On January 23, 2001, Clara was working at Miller's Country Store where she worked as a clerk one day a week. That day Ruby Bontrager came into the store to pick up some items. Ruby and Clara made small talk as Clara was ringing up Ruby's items. Ruby started telling Clara about her daughter who was in the process of adopting a child. Clara then shared with Ruby how she and Dennis had been thinking about adopting a child also. Before Ruby left, she offered Clara the phone number of the Goshen-Elkhart Agency. Clara said she would take it, and she put it into her pocket.

Another week went by and Clara thought, *Ah—we probably won't ever need this number. It's too much fuss to go through with adoption and besides, it takes money that we don't have.* With that thought, she threw away the paper. A week later Dennis brought up the subject again and said, "If we really want to do this, we aren't getting any younger. Sometimes it takes one to two years before things work out with adoption."

Clara replied, "Well, I threw the number away, but I could call Ruby and ask her for the number again." Dennis said he would like her to do that.

So Clara contacted Ruby Bontrager and got the number again. Immediately Clara called the Adoption Resource Services. Dennis and Clara made an appointment for their first interview—the following Monday, February 12, 2001. That day came and Dennis's schedule was filled to the max, so they decided to cancel the appointment. It was rescheduled for a week later on Monday, February 19, 2001, at 3:45 p.m.

The day of the interview Ruth Marks from Adoption Resource Services did the initial interview. Dennis and Clara arrived at the agency on time, driven by Aunt Lillian and Mother Mary Lou, along to run an errand. Ruth had told Dennis and Clara it would take around 1½-2 hours for the initial interview, so Mary Lou and Lillian went shopping. It wasn't long into the interview that Dennis and Clara sensed Ruth had something on her mind. She got up and went over to the window and said, "Yes, it's here." She came back, sat down, and started rubbing her hands on her skirt and then proceeded to say, "About fifteen minutes before you came (around 3:30 p.m.) we got a call from the social worker at Goshen Hospital. The social worker told us they have a girl that would like to place her child with an Amish couple." Ruth followed this statement with, "In all my sixteen years at the agency, I have never seen anything like this.

182

Never before has there been an Amish couple pursuing adoption here and never had a birthmother asked for an Amish couple like this one did." What was even more amazing, the call from the hospital came only fifteen minutes before Dennis and Clara arrived for their first interview!

Ruth Marks then proceeded to ask the question, "Would you be ready right now if this girl decides she wants to place with you?" Dennis and Clara's jaws fell open to their knees, and they looked at each other in amazement and then nodded. Ruth got up to get a Kleenex box, as this was too much for her. She gave Dennis and Clara some time to recover. She then asked them, "If this girl would like for you to come to the hospital, would you be able to do that?"

They replied, "Yes." Dennis and Clara left the agency with the agreement that they could expect a call from the agency sometime the next morning.

Dennis slept quite well that night, but sleep was hard to come by for Clara. Dennis checked the answering machine before he left for work at 6:00 a.m. There were no messages. He came back to the house and told Clara to check at 8:00 before she left for work. However, Clara could not contain herself, and she went out at 7:20 to check for messages. Again, there were no messages. At 9:00 a.m. Dennis checked again and still nothing. Clara checked at 10 a.m. and still nothing from the agency. At 11:40 Clara checked one more time, and there were three messages on the answering machine!

The first message was left at 10:19 a.m., soon after Clara had checked. The agency was getting frantic since they had not received a call from Dennis and Clara. They were going to close at noon in order for them to go to the hospital and go through paperwork with the birthmother. While Clara was on the phone with the agency, Lillian was driving past and noticed that Clara was on the phone. She stopped to talk with Clara. Ruth Marks wanted them to come to the hospital. She wanted to see them as soon as she was done meeting with the birthmother. So they got everything straightened out, and they arrived at the hospital at 3:00 p.m., Tuesday afternoon, February 20, 2001.

At this point Dennis and Clara were able to meet with the birthmother and some of her family. They had a nice visit with them. Dennis and Clara also were able to hold and rock the baby. However, it was still not set in stone as the birthmother had overnight to change her mind if this didn't suit her. Dennis and Clara were also given instructions to sleep over it and have the final answer by morning.

That Tuesday evening Dennis and Clara went around to different family members to share with them the sudden and overwhelming, yet exciting news! Doreen, Clara's sister, did not find peaceful sleep till the wee hours of the morning. Her adrenaline pumped her to the sewing machine and kept her going till after midnight. She still wasn't able to sleep well and before she knew it, it was time to get back up! This was just one example of the effect it left on Dennis and Clara's loved ones.

On Wednesday, Dennis and Clara arrived at the hospital around noon. It took most of the afternoon to get all the papers signed and for the doctor to come release the birthmother and the baby. Finally the hour came for the actual handing over of this precious gift.

Joy. Dennis was starting to think about this very important moment and felt in his mind he would like the birthmother to pick up her daughter and hand her to Clara when the actual parting took place.

In the meantime there was a knock on the door. The nurse came in and announced, "You have visitors." So Dennis and Clara went out to meet them and invite them in. It was Clara's folks. They noticed the birthmother going

184

over to the baby and picking her up. Clara's mom went over to the birthmother to talk to her and to give her a hug. At this point the birthmother starting talking to little Maria. She told her, "It's now time to say our good-byes. I know I haven't done right before God with my life." She went on to say she knows this is best for them both (birthmother and Maria) since she wouldn't be able to care for her like she would want to. The birthmother also said she believes this is God's will and plan for her to do this and then went on to tell Maria, "I'll come visit you in about a month." More kind and touching words were expressed to little Maria Joy by the birthmother.

After she was done talking to Maria Joy, she came over to Clara and handed the baby to her. It happened just as Dennis had pictured in his mind how he would like the exchange to take place. However, he had told no one of this. This was just one of many small incidents that made it so clear that the Lord Almighty was working and had arranged this whole thing by His mighty hand. God's presence was evident and felt so closely by everyone involved. The way everything fell into place made this event so special and meaningful. God worked out every detail.

It was like an angel handing over this baby to Clara when the mother put her in Clara's hands. Clara broke down and cried and all she could say through her tears was, "Thank you, thank you!" Dennis came over and took her in his arms, and together they wept with joy. They were so glad that Clara's folks were there to give their support. The awe and compassion everyone felt for the birthmother as she stood there with empty arms, kept the tears flowing. Clara overheard the birthmother say, "They are so overjoyed." The love Dennis and Clara (and all who were present) felt for the birthmother is the love we all want to feel for each other. This makes the love for their "newborn" child so wonderful and so real as this is their very own child to have and to cherish!

Next they all joined hands and Dennis led a prayer of deepest thanks for sharing His love with them and asked for strength and peace for the birthmother. This was a special bonding experience.

Dennis and Clara had a very positive adoption experience again when Amanda Grace was born. Friends told them about the birthmother. After interaction with the birthmother and her family, she chose Dennis and Clara to be the baby's parents. Clara and the birthmother had both chosen Amanda to be the baby's name.

After one positive experience with Dennis and Clara, Maria's birthmother again chose them to parent her baby. She presented them with the gift of another daughter on September 5, 2003. Together they named her Sandra Hope. Dennis and Clara's empty arms are now filled with three special little girls.

20

Lester & Mattie Yoder

Regina Ann — *February 10, 1997*

—Topeka, Indiana

We are Amish and live on a farm in northern Indiana. Lester also works at Redmon, a mobile home factory and reupholsters furniture. In 1989 we started taking in foster children to fill the void in our home. We preferred to have under-school-aged children, but occasionally had teenagers for short periods of time. We had about 42 or 43 children in 10 years' time. We never really talked about adopting children, but some of the younger babies we really got attached to, and it just broke our hearts when they went back, and yet we knew it was changing! We had one baby girl from the time she was three months old until she was nearly three years old. The social worker realized how hard this was on me, as twice in the time we had her they said the parental rights would be terminated, but it never happened.

In February of 1997, a baby girl was born in LaGrange Hospital who was available for adoption right away. They came and told us we have first chance.

We were allowed to name her, and we named her Regina Ann. We felt this was an answer to prayers, and the joy to think she could stay here! This was a closed adoption, but we would be willing to help Regina find her birthmother if she wants to someday. We took a lot of training during the years we were fostering children, which had helped us a lot. Due to health conditions we are no longer fostering, but would gladly adopt another one if the Lord sees it for our good. Both sides of the families have really accepted Regina as part of the family and have made her feel welcome wherever she is! She has lots of little cousins to play with, which she enjoys! God bless all who wish to adopt these innocent children.

From Anxiety and Darkness

From anxiety and darkness
Comes a ray of shining light.
You've sent a precious child to us,
O God of Wonder and of Might.

You know how much the wanting
And you know how long the wait,
But from all of this frustration,
Comes a joy, that's oh, so great!

We felt Your presence all around us,
And we know You truly care
When we look into this tiny crib
And see our baby lying there.

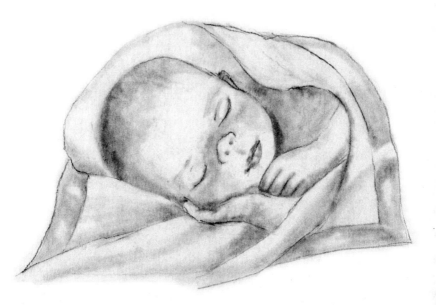

You've made another miracle
Which came to us today.
You've given us this special child
Who's now forever home to stay.

How thankful we are this minute—
Our prayers have all come true.
We're a family through adoption,
And we owe it all to You.

Written by Mary Jane Proft.
Reprinted with permission of *Mary Sue Originals*.

21

Sim & Sara Yoder

Laura — *June 6, 1975*
Ray — *September 17, 1976*
Donald — *May 7, 1968*
David — *March 12, 1971*
Phyllis — *March 1, 1979*
Karen — *July 25, 1980*
Joyce — *February 16, 1983*
Elizabeth — *February 13, 1986*
Paul — *March 22, 1988*
Mark — *February 22, 1990*
Kathy — *April 11, 1992*
Lamar — *September 11, 1995*

—Dublin, Georgia

Sara and I married in July of 1974 and lived at Hephzibah, Georgia, for a year and a half. Our oldest daughter Laura was born there. We moved to Dublin in December of 1975 and in September 1976 our second child Ray was born. Time moved on and in August of 1978 we were visiting Sara's home at Pensacola and visited one of her classmates who had two boys—Donald, 10, and David, 7. As it worked out we were to take the boys home with us to Georgia for a vacation. This was the beginning of the relationship with

191

the boys, which made them third and fourth for our family. In March of 1979 Phyllis joined the family, then Karen in July of 1980 and Joyce in February of 1983. Elizabeth (Libby) made number eight and arrived in February of 1986, number nine was Paul in March of 1988, and Mark was number ten arriving in March of 1990. Kathy arrived in April of 1992 making eleven. Last but not least is number twelve, Lamar, arriving on September 11, 1995. That makes the lineup.

As you can see, the first six years of our marriage were busy ones with six children in that amount of time. We called it instant family. We have lived on a farm from day one of our marriage, so there was nearly always plenty for everyone to do. Church life was always a big part of our life. We are a part of the Pilgrim Mennonite Conference, members at the Dublin congregation.

The story goes back to the early 1970s when Sara was in nurses' training in Pensacola, and became friends with a girl called Sally. Sally wanted to do right but never had the will to step out for God and put the old life behind. During this time the friendship between Sara and Sally grew, and also Sara noticed the two little boys that she was "dragging" into an ungodly lifestyle. In this time period Sally went through a divorce and then remarried. By the summer of 1978 her words were that she wanted the boys to have a better opportunity in life than she did. She wanted them to be raised in a Christian home, and remembered Sara as a godly young girl from school, and wanted us to take the boys to Georgia for a vacation. Before the week was over, she agreed that the boys could just stay with us.

It is only natural that all of mankind wants to know who brought them into the world, and we think that to be open with the adopted child on the subject will build appreciation and trust. To try to keep everything quiet tends to do otherwise. Adopted children need a healthy love for the birthparents and then a healthy love will grow for their adopted parents. We should cultivate a love for the ones who brought them into the world. They will not love the adoptive parents less because of a healthy love for the biological parent.

Donald enjoyed playing games as most youth do; trapping and hunting were big things to him. As he grew, he began to notice a young girl that was teaching our school. Joan Weaver was from Illinois. Well, it didn't go too long until we were looking for another teacher and Donald stopped looking for a wife. She is a wonderful wife for him and a good daughter-in-law. They were married in May 1988, and now have ten children. The oldest one is a member of the church here too.

David met Cheryl Mast, whose parents had moved to Mexico in church work. Our family went to Mexico in 1990 and this is when they started courting. We went back in 1991 for the wedding. They live about three miles from us and have five children. Cheryl is a wonderful wife for him, and good mother and daughter-in-law too. If all of our children get companions as good as Donald and David have, we will be richly blessed.

Donald and David are both members here and active in the church. They both have a desire to raise their families for the Lord. We are so grateful to God for His goodness to us over the years. We are glad they are part of our family. I'm glad that in the summer of 1978 we made that little decision of taking two boys on a little vacation, and God stayed with us the rest of the way.

Adoption–Second Best?

by Carol Chaney, M.D., Harrison, AR

In some recent discussion with Christian acquaintances about adoption, someone commented, "Well, you know, I just wouldn't want to do that. I'd rather have my own flesh and blood. An adopted child would just be second best."

My comment was, "If that is your attitude, please spare the child a selfish parent and a dreadful future of being treated as second best, and don't adopt."

As I reflect on this attitude existing in persons who are serious in their commitment as Christians and would never think about missing church when the doors are open, I have felt astonishment, anger, sadness, and finally the need to address the subject.

When one looks at adoption from a Biblical perspective, we find that God has adopted those who accept Jesus as Saviour. Romans 8:15-17 says, "For ye have not received the spirit of bondage again to fear; but ye have received the *Spirit of adoption*, whereby we cry, Abba, Father. The Spirit itself beareth witness with our spirit, that we are the children of God: and if children, then heirs; heirs of God, and joint-heirs with Christ; if so be that we suffer with him, that we may be also glorified together."

In Galatians 4:4-7, we find that "when the fulness of the time was come, God sent forth his Son, made of a woman, made under the law, to redeem them that were under the law, that we might receive *the adoption of sons.* And because ye are sons, God hath sent forth the Spirit of his Son into your hearts, crying, Abba, Father. Wherefore thou art no more a servant, but a son; and if a son, than an heir of God through Christ."

In Ephesians 1:5 we see that He has "predestinated us unto *the adoption of children* by Jesus Christ to himself, according to the good pleasure of his will."

In John 1:12, 13, we are told that "as many as received him, to them gave he power to become the sons of God, even to them that believe on his name: which were born, *not of blood*, nor of the will of the flesh, nor of the will of man, but of God."

Finally, in Romans 8:23, the Holy Spirit nudges Paul to write: "And not only they [created animals and plants suffering in sickness], but ourselves also, which have the firstfruits of the Spirit, even we ourselves groan within ourselves, waiting for the *adoption*, to wit, the redemption of our body."

As I look at these verses, I wonder how anyone can truly have a "second best" attitude about adoption, when the only reason we as Christians have any hope of salvation is by accepting the vision that through Christ's death, God has truly adopted each of us as His child. Does God consider us second best? Somehow, I don't think that Christ's life of service, suffering, and an agonizing death on earth was given to us so that we could be second-class children.

The human desire to have children is certainly understandable, but whether they arrive by biology or through adoption should not really make a difference, if we are Christians.

In recent discussion with a gracious and humble Christian lady who has raised several biological and adopted children, we discussed this issue. Why is it that some people are able to go beyond natural human selfishness and truly love other people's offspring as their own "flesh and blood"? Perhaps we cannot answer that. But I observe this: One must have a genuine love for children above self.

Adoption must be undertaken because of love for the children and not because of fulfilling a duty or a checklist of good deeds. One's attitude has to be right. Nothing—not

196

even a noble-sounding purpose—will work out right if it is done to honor self. Once our lives have been truly given to the Lord and we seek His guidance, not our will, then our hearts are open to more than selfish desire.

I sometimes wonder if we women in particular tend to place children and family above God. And if a woman has no children, we wonder, "What is her role in life?" Does society, Christian or not, treat a childless woman with less respect than one with children?

Do some people have children mostly to satisfy a personal need for significance? If so, we might say, "Look at me, I did a good job taking care of my family." If that's the goal, then it's enough to have a home with a nice picket fence, two parents, and happy siblings. It allows no interruptions to a perfect setting with the right round of church, ice cream socials, occasional "do-good" deeds for those outside our sphere of perfection and comfort, and, oh yes, offerings, donations, and socially acceptable good deeds and words.

But what about taking a chance and making a sacrifice? What about taking a child into our home and loving, teaching, disciplining, feeding, clothing, and guiding that child prayerfully? Why have we not considered this more often? One person, one couple, or even one church cannot save all the homeless children in the world. But one person or one couple can make a difference in his or her own corner by sharing his/her good fortune with a child who desperately needs simply to be loved and to belong to a family. When I experienced what I did some eight years ago, the blinders just wouldn't stay on my eyes and heart and I knew more of God's love after the encounters I will now tell you about:

Jorge (pronounced hor-hay) was eleven years old. Being one of the older children at the orphanage in La Cuidad Victoria, Mexico, he was outgrowing the cute stage of childhood and was already aware of a harshness in life that we comfortable Americans would never want our grown children, much less our eleven-year-olds, exposed to. During my month of visiting and helping at the orphanage, Jorge had overcome some of his shyness and would want to talk to me and tell me about himself. He would draw pictures and give them to me and often would just want to walk about and hold my hand when the younger ones were not in my lap.

One day, shortly before my departure, he came to me with tears in his eyes and asked me to take a gift home with me so I would remember him. My gift was to be the only physical possession he had in this world. He kept it in a shoe box beneath his bed—his treasure—a wooden cup-and-ball toy. Jorge proudly handed the precious toy to me in his hand that was missing two fingers due to a cruel knife cut, early in life. As I fought back tears and gave him a hug, the disparity of our worlds hung like a heavy, invisible weight upon my heart. My mind could not conceive of a child being willing to give up his only personal possession to someone like me, who was only passing through his life for a few weeks. I wanted to say no, but his eyes were gazing directly into mine, looking for acceptance and love. His eyes bravely pleaded to belong in some way to this stranger who tried to speak his language, listened to his stories, kept his pictures, and held his crippled hand. After meeting that gaze, I accepted his gift with a simple, "Thank you, Jorge. I shall always remember you and your kindness."

And then there was David, a small, wiry, mischievous ten-year-old. David had the attention span and activity level of a bumblebee. He was definitely "buzzy" and often in trouble. But he had the most endearing nature and for a few minutes after a spanking, really did try to do better. David, too, was frequently at my side, holding my hand and wanting me to read to him. During one of these reading sessions, he asked me if I could please take him home with me so he could have

198

a family and we could read every day. On my last day at the orphanage he hung onto me off and on the whole day, crying and asking me to please take him and to be his mother.

These eight years have passed since I saw Jorge and David. They are now grown and have left the orphanage. I do not know where they are or what they are doing. But I am grateful to them for the lessons they taught me.

They showed me the wonder of sharing love—of giving. They returned to me a thousandfold my gift of time and effort. Their gifts to me were rich with bright smiles and hugs, tears on dust-smeared faces saying, "Thank you" and "Good-bye." I hope those children's memories of me someday will bring them a bit closer to God, as my memories of them have done for me. If anyone could spend time with children who need love and a home and then walk away, saying, "I prefer my own flesh and blood to this second-best," it seems to me the devil dressed in a cold cloak of selfishness must be dwelling in such a heart.

Looking at Mark 9:36, 37, we find, "And he took a child, and set him in the midst of them: and when he had taken him in his arms, he said unto them, Whosoever shall receive one of such children in my name, receiveth me: and whosoever shall receive me, receiveth not me, but him that sent me." In Mark 9:42, "And whosoever shall offend one of these little ones that believe in me, it is better for him that a millstone were hanged about his neck, and he were cast into the sea."

How many of us can honestly say that we have welcomed a little child into our lives as God adopted and welcomed us? Even animals in the wild ferociously defend their "flesh and blood" young, so our own animal instinct of caring for and defending our own "flesh and blood" is perhaps not so much noble as it is instinctive. If, as Christians, we look at each other as brothers and sisters, why do we not make more of an effort to bring children who need us desperately into our homes and arms as family, and thereby welcome our Father in heaven?

Looking at adoption from a more temporal view—financially and legally—the reality of the difficulty of adoption becomes real. It is often expensive and the time and frustration of paperwork and social welfare home checks can be daunting. But when one compares the hundreds of thousands of dollars which can be involved in infertility workups and premature births (which occur more frequently with fertility drugs), why not pursue adoption at an earlier point in weighing one's options?

Have any churches or other organizations ever considered sponsoring an adoption fund to help couples give a home to a child? In comparing medical costs of hundreds of thousands of dollars to ten or twenty thousand for routine adoption, the cost does not seem prohibitive at all.

Mr. Dave Thomas, who started Wendy's restaurant chain, started the Dave Thomas Foundation for Adoption. He himself was adopted and understood the depth of how being given to a good home can affect one's life. He created a program to encourage and assist his employees with adoption. Why can't we as Christian groups and organizations do the same?

To sum it up in a short statement that my four-year-old son once said to me, "Now, Mama, you better go sit and *fink* about *dat*" (think about that). At the present age of 13 years, he has been through several scoldings, hugs, book readings, swimming lessons, music lessons, early morning and late evening homework sessions, and many more experiences.

The sweetest words to my ears are still, "Mama, you are the BEST mama, well, most of the time, and I love you higher than the sky."

My son happens to be adopted. First class doesn't get better than that.

200

22

Delbert & Brenda Martin

—Goshen, Indiana

Adult Adoptee–Brenda's story

I'm Brenda Martin, an adopted daughter of Kenneth and Susie Zimmerman. Susie passed away in December 2000. Kenneth is married again to Lydia Huber. Lydia is like a mother to me now.

I can't really say that my life was any different or more extraordinary than anyone else's life. We were just a normal family. I've many times been thankful for the opportunities that I've had. My parents were very good about making no distinction between me and their biological children.

I was born on May 15, 1963, back when they did not give out information on adoptions. I really don't know anything about my biological parents, but it really doesn't matter. There were times that I have wondered who they were, but yet with having a happy life, I never wished to go find my birthparents. I was content with my home and my life. My dad told me they were interviewed by the Department of Welfare. They wanted to know their background. They were told they would try to match a baby with them that would probably fit to them better than some others as far as a background. That's the most I would ever know about it.

Kenneth and Susie were married five years before their first son was born. It went five years later before they adopted me, then four years later when another son was born, then followed two more daughters. They went into

201

foster parenting. That is when they adopted my two youngest brothers. There were seven of us children and we were all one family. I never felt that I was treated or accepted any different than the other children.

I think being adopted is a privilege that not everyone has. I had to think if I wouldn't have been adopted, I wouldn't have the husband and children I have. Also I would probably not have been raised in a Christian home or had the parents, friends, teachers, ministers, church family, etc.

Delbert, my husband, has been a real encouragement to me. Yellow Creek Wisler Mennonite is our home church. We have five children: Stacy Lynn born September 4, 1984;

Delbert Martin family

Justin Rendell born March 17, 1987; Shanda Janee born June 20, 1991; Dalton Ray born August 31, 1995; and Brandon Kyle born February 15, 2001.

It doesn't matter if we're adopted or not. We all need to be responsible for decisions we make in our life. We will all need to answer to God someday when life is over. We can't use the excuse that we're adopted and feel sorry for ourselves, just so we can do what we want. I think if we look at it with a positive attitude it will be a benefit to us and we or you will find many blessings.

To all adoptive parents: Thank you for being caring and sharing your homes. Your children do need you.

Maybe we need to look at it from the adoptive parents' angle. We don't know or have any idea how empty your arms feel. We are thankful for you, even if sometimes we make you wonder!

Hoping that someday we as adopted children and our families and everyone else can be one big family in heaven.

23

Roger & Joy Rangai

Adult Adoptee–Joy's story

A *home at last.* "It has to be in here," said Papa John, as he quickly scanned his slides. He had just finished a wonderful slide presentation to our little group that consisted of my newly-wedded wife, her parents, and me. We were at his home that evening for supper and this occasion. It was focused primarily on the AMA Children's Home that once existed in El Salvador. Now he was desperately searching for one more slide.

Beside me, my wife sat quietly, but nervous. In her excitement she was breathing rapidly, for she, too, had guessed what picture it was. Then all at once Papa John stopped! My wife's hands flew to her mouth, then back down again. Before us on the screen stood a little seven-year-old girl in a short and faded dress that she had now outgrown. Her hair was cut and in disarray. In her hands she clung to a rag doll. But most noticeably were her eyes that told of much loneliness, rejection, and lack of love in her life.

After a moment's pause Papa John spoke up. "This is it," he said. "This is what I was looking for all evening. And this is the way she looked when we brought her from the 'Rosa Virginia.' What you see in this picture was everything she owned."

Brother John Mast (or Papa John, as he is fondly called by the now-adopted children he once worked with) was referring to a little girl by the name of Maria Celina Porraz, one of nearly three hundred homeless and unwanted children that were in the hands of the juvenile court of El Salvador to care for, even though they were unable to do so properly. These children were housed in a girls' observatory and a

Roger Rangai family

boys' reformatory known as the "Rosa Virginia."

In 1972 the Lord made the way clear for the AMA Mission to open the doors of "New Life and Hope" orphanage in El Salvador. This children's home immediately began to fill a great need for that country's many children that were neglected and forsaken. Three years later, in 1975, while John Mast served as director, Maria was transferred to this orphanage. Thus began a great change in her life from a situation of hopelessness and many unpleasant experiences to a time of new life and hope! Thirteen months later, at the age of eight years, she made the joyful trip with her new parents, David L. and Edna Miller, to her new home in Goshen, Indiana. Her new name was now Joy Maria Miller. At the age of fourteen she accepted Christ as her personal Saviour. Ten years later on August 24, 1991, Joy became my wife and God has since blessed us with five lovely children that she can shower with all the love and care that she missed as a child. Our children are: Steven, born May 8, 1992; Carlos, born September 24, 1993; Rhonda, born December 20, 1995; Angela, born September 2, 1998; Edwin, born August 24, 2001.

How the Story Began. There are many details of how this story began that we may never know on this side of eternity. Naturally, one's life story begins at birth, but Joy knows nothing of her birth. She faintly remembers a woman that was probably her mother. What she does remember is that she lived with her grandma, and she knew she was there because her mother did not want her, but neither did her grandma. There are many memories of her life with Grandma that are so painful, they are best forgotten. Perhaps Grandma's life was simply a reflection of a larger society that had degraded to a state of immorality and emptiness, devoid of understanding, and very little knowledge of the love of God. Judging from Grandma's behavior, sanctity of life was almost nonexistent and the selfish desires of most people ruled their lives. Children were therefore a nuisance and unwanted objects in their path, which in turn brought about many kinds of child abuse.

There were three other children at Grandma's place, that were probably siblings to Joy. To these children and to Grandma she bonded, and this was the only family she knew in her early childhood. Grandma took care of them, but she had a mean temper, and because she did not want them, she threatened many times to kill them all. At one time she caught hold of Maria (Joy's name before she was adopted) and wrapped her fingers around her throat, probably squeezing with intention to choke her to death. Maria squirmed and wiggled and kicked enough that she somehow managed to get away and she fled. When Maria was finally handed over to the "Rosa Virginia," there were only two other children besides herself. Where was the fourth one? Did Grandma actually carry out her murder threats on child number four? We do not know.

Grandma had pierced Maria's ears and strung a thread through until her ears healed, intending to put earrings on her. But Maria did not want earrings, so she pulled on the threads and literally tore her ears apart to get them out. This furiously enraged Grandma. She picked up a broom and chased after Maria. When she caught her she commenced to maul her on the head with the broomstick, but Maria again broke loose from her grip. Another time when Grandma chased her with a stick, Maria's little legs outran her. So Grandma threw a glass bottle at her head, but missed. Once when Maria misbehaved, Grandma pulled her hair quite firmly as punishment. Grandma soon had enough. Information received from the children's homes indicates that Maria was taken to her aunt's place, but trouble soon ensued there because Maria could not get along with her little cousin. Their solution to the problem was to take her to "Rosa Virginia."

Nightmare at Rosa Virginia. One day Grandma and Maria went for a walk with Maria's aunt and the other children (child number four was mysteriously not along). Their walk ended at the "Rosa Virginia." After awhile, without realizing what was happening, Maria saw her grandma starting down the road on her way back home. What was she doing? Was she planning on leaving her at this place? Immediately her heart ripped wide open. She screamed and ran after her shouting, "*Abuela! Abuela!* (Grandma! Grandma!)" Grandma simply waited for her and gave her a sound spanking, then took her back to the "Rosa Virginia." This time she gave her some candy to sweeten her up and took her to a room where she would not see her leave. That was the last time she saw her grandma, her aunt, and the children she had known. All her objects of security were gone. The children she had played with, eaten with, slept with, she never saw anymore. She was now in a large, dirty building with over a hundred other girls, yet she was extremely lonely. Can you explain the grief of a five- or six-year-old that has just been stripped of everything she owned and trusted in, even though that security was really no security at all?

Life at the "Rosa Virginia" was a nightmare from the start. Controlling over a hundred girls that are all searching for love and belonging would certainly be a discouraging job.

One of Maria's jobs was helping clean the bathrooms that were very unsanitary and repulsive. Privacy was impossible and left many unpleasant memories. Another chore was hauling many buckets of water every day for bathrooms and cleaning the floor as well as dumping on the ground outside to keep the dust down.

A Change Begins. Approximately two months after John Masts took over as administrators at "New Life and Hope" orphanage, the request came from "Rosa Virginia" for them to consider taking three more of their children. One of those children was Maria. The Masts went over to get the children, accompanied by Daniel Bontragers (who did the legal work at the home). There they found Maria, severely infested with lice and clutching a doll. These children had been deceived, abused, and mistreated. This is the doll that Maria was holding in the picture at John Masts.

At the "New Life and Hope" orphanage a whole new world opened up for Maria. Here she found love and care like she had never experienced before. There was a devotional time in the morning and mealtimes were a joy. There were clean clothes to wear and clean facilities. There was schooltime with a caring schoolteacher!

There was one thing that came as a surprise to Maria, but it turned out to be a pleasant surprise. That was discipline! She discovered that order and obedience were requirements here. But when discipline was administered, it was done in love. It made her feel wanted and loved. Slowly, healing began to take effect, because a disciplined life certainly makes life more meaningful.

Why did God bring Maria to this children's home when hundreds of other children were denied the privilege? I am sure God knew that one day this little girl would grow up and become my wife! What an all-knowing and caring God that leads us every step of the way!

Today there are many children in the States who came from "New Life and Hope" and were adopted into Christian homes. Not all have been faithful to God, but I believe all have fond memories of the AMA children's home because they were like one big, happy family. When these children meet today, and one starts a conversation about the children's home, I simply have to listen quietly, because I have nothing to say. And even if I would want to say something, I couldn't, because they get so excited when they reminisce.

The Millers. David L. and Edna Miller were blessed with six children. Three of them had started homes of their own and the youngest was almost a teenager. They were already past fifty years old but they developed a yearning for another child. What gave them this yearning? When I first met David (now my father-in-law) I was at once impressed with his unselfishness and love for people. He was willing to go out of his way to make me feel at home. I believe Maria saw this as well when she first met them. Davids knew Daniel Bontragers well, since they lived not far from each other. So that gave them a place to start in their search for another child. At this time Daniels were in El Salvador helping with the administrative work at "New Life and Hope." After a lot of correspondence and legal work they were finally ready to go after their seventh child! In January 1976, Dad and Mom Miller, accompanied by Uncle Ammon and Aunt Girtie (Dad's sister) flew to El Salvador for this very special occasion.

Meanwhile at the children's home, Maria, like all the other children, was longing for a home to belong to. The ones that were never adopted felt useless because they decided nobody wanted them. Maria's heart leapt for joy when she learned she was getting a dad and mom. She was now eight years old. They sent her pictures of her future family—Dad and Mom, three sisters and three brothers, besides a bonus of two sisters-in-law, one brother-in-law, and five nephews! She would live on a farm in a beautiful house and have lots of cows to help milk.

When she went to the airport to meet Dad and Mom, she immediately flew into their arms and would not let them get out of sight for the whole length of their stay in El Salvador. She was even allowed to stay in their cabin at the home. Dad and Mom wanted to visit the "Rosa Virginia." When they arrived there, Maria was terrified! She clung to Mom and screamed, for she was afraid of being left there again.

Adjustments. Maria Celina Porras was leaving El Salvador with her new parents and a new name as well. "You are such a joy to us," said Mom. "We will name you Joy Maria. So now you are our Joy Maria Miller." Of course, this was perfectly okay.

Joy and her sister Sharon discovered one of the first adjustments they had to make. It happened after they were in bed the first night she was at home. The problem was that Sharon spoke Pennsylvania Dutch and Joy spoke Spanish. Sharon lovingly told her new sister, *"Du bisht vacha!"* (You are awake!) Joy was very offended. *"No soy un vaca!"* (I am not a cow!), she said indignantly. But Sharon was insistent, *"Yo, du bisht vacha!"* (Yes, you are awake!) Then Joy, "No, I am Joy! I am not a cow!" She had learned some English at the home just before she was adopted, but Pennsylvania Dutch was completely new. For awhile she had all three languages mixed together which made it difficult to communicate with her. Today she is fluent in Pennsylvania Dutch and English, but she has lost all her Spanish.

Despite the adjustments, Joy adapted perfectly into the Miller home. Dad was firm in not making a distinction between his biological children and adopted child. Furthermore, the church, school, and extended family did an excellent job in making Joy feel welcome and one of them.

Today Joy knows beyond any shadow of doubt where she belongs. She has no desire to go back to the family that rejected and disowned her. My mind goes back to an incident soon after we were married and moved to Belize. Joy was fighting homesickness like new brides do occasionally. She lay on the bed and cried, "I want Mom! I want Mom!" I think of the time much earlier in her life when she shouted heartbrokenly, *"Abuela! Abuela!"* However this time she knew her mom would never leave her. She had given her all the love and care that any child could wish for.

212

Joy now has her dad and mom, a husband, two daughters, and three sons. All her brothers and sisters are married, providing her with many nieces and nephews. She loves to talk about her family. She can name many first, second, and third cousins that are seemingly scattered all over the United States.

My family are all in Belize, Central America, and consists of five sisters, four brothers, and my dad. They all have families except one and my dad is alone since Mom passed away nine years ago. We feel so blessed to have large families on both sides. Most of all we are blessed to be a part of the family of God! At present we are members at Faith Mennonite Church in Lott, Texas. This has been home for the last five years until the Lord directs otherwise. Joy stays busy with housekeeping and being a good neighbor to those around us. I work at a lawn furniture shop nearby and part-time at home. Three of our children are in school. God has been good to us and I have the assurance from His Word that He will continue to bless us.

Are there any scars in the life of an adopted child? When we receive a newborn baby that was born to us, we have, as it were, a clean slate to begin with. But in the life of an adopted child, we must also help to erase the past and start afresh.

The next time we see someone that was adopted, may God help us to feel with them, may we help to heal their unfortunate past, which is caused many times by the sin and evil around us, then may we rejoice with them that God has made something beautiful out of their lives. May this also stir our hearts for the many children that would love to belong to a home where peace and love abounds and God is there.

Joy's testimony can be summed up in the words of the song: "From the door of an orphanage, To the house of the King— No longer an outcast, Now a new song I sing. I'm so glad I'm a part of the family of God!"

The Life of a Child
Without a Mother

Chorus: The life of a child without a mother,
          Is like cookies with no batter.
          The life of a child without a mother,
          Is like rungs with no ladder.
          The life of a child without a mother
          Is a life of being alone.
          The life of a child without a mother,
          It is the saddest I've ever known.

          The little boy sees the robin
          Caring for her nest,
          Always giving her young ones
          What she knows is best.
          With trembling lips he asks his daddy,
          Why are the birds more blest?
          Why can't I have a mama?
          Just like all the rest?

          In the darkness, someone is crying,
          Wetting the pillow 'neath his head.
          As again and again he reaches
          For the empty side of the bed.
          God only knows the agony
          Of this man's broken heart,
          With a family of children
          Whose mother wants no part.

So many youth let their lives be guided
By hopes and dreams of romance.
When their hearts begin to flutter
They drop the guard and take the chance.
Always pray about tomorrow,
Before you set your goals;
Future mamas and future daddies
You must consider those little souls.

—by Lavern Stoll
Conneautville, PA

When Lavern was a young boy, his mother left his father with a family of seven young children. Many heartaches were caused through this, and thus this song was born.

Lavern married Ella Troyer in 1985, and God blessed them with four children—three biological, and one through adoption from China.

They are members of the Conneautville New Order Church. Lavern works as a maintenance man at J. N. Pallet Company.

24

Rodney & Jeanne Witmer

—Flora Vista, New Mexico

Adult Adoptee—Jeanne's story

Rodney and I, with our five sons—Austin, Carlin, Nolan, Jaren, and Wendon—live in the Farmington, New Mexico area. Rodney is a cabinetmaker by trade. We are members of the Farmington Mennonite Church. Rodney is bishop of the church here.

I entered the William Cross family as a newborn baby. I am very thankful that my parents chose to adopt me and gave me a Christian home to grow up in. I shudder to think where I could be if I hadn't had this chance. But I cannot say that it was all a bed of roses. I had a lot of struggles that I bottled up inside of me. Why didn't I talk about it to someone? Because I didn't want anybody to think of me as being different from others, I always hoped people didn't know it. My family was very nice about it and didn't talk about it much. When it came up by necessity, they always were very quick to assure me that I was one of the family.

When my birthmother died of cancer, I had the opportunity to meet one of my half-sisters. I refused because I had my own family and didn't want the confusion of having to deal with two families and be different from my friends.

I was always a little worried that a boy wouldn't want to date me when he discovered that I was adopted. It was reassuring when Rodney asked me, because I knew he already knew and accepted me for who I was.

217

I used to cringe when I heard people outside the family talk about me. I hated it! I didn't want to be different, even if they thought it was wonderful that I was adopted and part of the family.

I think it is wonderful now too. I marvel at God's plan for each one's life and how He brings it to pass. I think it is wonderful too, that there are families that open their hearts and homes to little ones and give them love and a chance to grow up in a Christian home. May the Lord richly bless your efforts and may it only bring you joy.

25

Eli & Leanna Yutzy

—Topeka, Indiana

Adult Adoptee–Leanna's story

We are members of the Old Order Amish Church. My husband is Eli Yutzy, son of Norman and Ida Yutzy, of Bloomfield, Iowa. My parents are Floyd and Wilma Bontrager. Eli and I have four biological children: Marcus Lynn, age ten; Julie Diane, age nine; Darin Michael, age five; and Bethany Jane, age one.

I was brought to my parents' home right out of the hospital at four days old. I cannot remember being told that I'm adopted; therefore I'd assume I was too young to remember it, or maybe it was just something we always talked about openly. I do remember as a child longing more than anything to have a baby brother or sister. Someone to play with, yes, but also I think in my mind that would have made me more like other children and kept me from being labeled as different. Everyone in school knew I was an only child, and was certainly spoiled (or so they thought)! I suppose in a way I was. I had privileges the other children didn't. But what they didn't realize was, they had privileges I didn't have— someone to talk to, play with, and who would stick up for them, no matter what. Children can be cruel in their innocence. They tend to repeat what they hear from their parents. I would encourage them not to mention that this or that child is adopted; at least not until their children are old enough to understand what adoption really means.

219

I think feeling "different" has changed somewhat since I'm older, with children of my own now. But there are still times when I feel I don't quite fit in here in our church and community. I do sometimes long to find this woman that gave birth to me. I hesitate to call her mother since I have a mom who is all I could ever wish for. What I share with my adoptive parents goes beyond sharing the same blood. To me they are my real parents and always will be! No one could ever fill that spot in my heart that I have reserved for my "parents." I cannot ever thank God enough for the privilege of calling them "Mom and Dad."

A Tribute to Adoptive Parents

Parents are special, each and every one.
They take care of us when we're little,
Teach us right when we're young.
But not all parents are quite like mine—
These wonderful people, so loving and kind.
I was four days old when I came to their home,
Wrinkled and crying and very alone.
But I was so blessed that God sent me there
To this wonderful home, to people who care.
And to this day it doesn't matter, you see,
For they are <u>my real</u> parents, so precious to me.
We don't share the same blood, as most families do,
But they're my real Mom and Dad, I'd do anything for you.
This is to tell you, Mom and Dad, that I love you more
Than any parents I could have had.
I don't feel "adopted" because of you two.
You gave me a life
For that I say "Thank You."

by Leanna Yutzy

Our Family Tree

We've added to our family tree,
A stronger one to make.
A child from another plant
Has become our new namesake.

Just as a limb is grafted
From one tree to another,
It alters and improves the plant,
Making it uniquely like no other.

Our family tree has been improved,
Adoption made this so.
For love, much more than bloodlines,
Makes us thrive and grow.

We chose to share our life and love
And all the joys to come.
Our "family tree" has blossomed
With the arrival of our cherished one.

Written by Mary Jane Proft.
Reprinted with permission of *Mary Sue Originals*.

26

LeRoy & Velma Schrock

—Goshen, Indiana

Grandparents' story—Rhoda Bontrager's parents

We have learned adoption is not an easy way for a childless couple to have someone to call them Mama and Daddy. For most couples, it is a roller-coaster experience. The couple (and the grandparents) can be anxiously waiting only to be dealt another disappointment. We were privileged to be involved with the adoption experience of our daughter and her husband, Thomas and Rhoda Bontrager. Sometimes it was "Weep with them that weep," and four times we could "rejoice with them that do rejoice." Those times we certainly felt this child was meant to be theirs and to be our grandchild.

We don't consider the "born to" or the "born for" grandchildren any different. Each one has a very special place in our hearts and lives.

We feel grateful that some single girls were careful in their consideration and chose to place their baby in a two-parent home where they can grow up in a sound, stable, Christian home. It is those girls who realize their sweet, tiny baby will grow up to need more than they can give. It is not that they don't want or love the child, but they love it enough to want the best for the child. Many a young girl has chosen to parent her baby, but when it is no longer sweet and innocent, neglects and abuses it, only to have it taken away by an agency. The child often ends up carrying emotional scars and scenes they should never have known.

Our grandchildren look so much like their parents; many people find it hard to believe they weren't biologically born. They were happy with every one the Lord chose for them. They have two boys and two girls with spacing in years like other families.

No matter how our grandchildren come into our family, they are wanted, loved, and prayed for. Our desire is for each one to choose to serve the Lord.

Some of our adopted grandchildren we eagerly awaited for, but the last one came as a big surprise! The three older ones were praying for a baby when the phone rang telling them they had a baby sister.

It was a highlight in our lives to have two granddaughters in four days! One anticipated, and one a surprise!

When an aunt asked the three-year-old, "May I take the baby home," he promptly answered, "We prayed for this one, you can pray for one yourself!" That aunt was carefully watched for some time to make sure she wouldn't take the baby!

It hurts us when people point out and make special note that, "they are adopted," giving the impression they are different and less valuable. Not so. The Lord gives His blessings in various ways, and our adopted grandchildren have been a special blessing.

Sometimes people ask about their real mother, which is rather a silly question. The birthmother gave life and birth; the adoptive mother loves, cares, and provides for them the remainder of their lives, so who is the real mother?

27

Homer & Etta Schwartz

—Goshen, Indiana

Grandparents' story—Karen Mast's parents

After our marriage, God blessed us with seven healthy children—four girls and three boys. We now realize, as we look back, that we took our children too much for granted. Adopting children on our part was not necessary for us to discuss or consider, etc.

After our oldest daughter and husband were married we assumed that they would have children too. But as time went on and no children were born, the question now came up about adoption. Our response was rather negative at first, and we weren't much help to them at this point. But after hearing their stories of other couples, their experiences, and seeing their eagerness to have children to love and care for, we began to reconsider and consented to support them—by praying, encouraging, and traveling with them each time.

They now have three children—two boys and one girl. They have spent a lot of money, traveled many miles, and faced disappointments. But they are happy and enjoy a sense of fulfillment in all this. God has been good to them and us and especially to these young innocent little souls (oldest one, five). They are still too young to realize what a tremendous opportunity they now have to grow up (Lord willing) in a normal Christian home, and how different it would have been for them, if someone had not loved them and

225

cared for them in this way.

We encourage other adoptive grandparents to support their children (and grandchildren) if adopting children for their own is what they choose.

You Are Who You Are

You are who you are for a reason.
You're part of an intricate plan.
You're a precious and perfect unique design,
Called God's special woman or man.

You look like you look for a reason.
Our God made no mistake.
He knit you together within the womb,
You're just what He wanted to make.

The parents you had were the ones He chose,
And no matter how you may feel,
They were custom-designed with God's plan in mind,
And they bear the Master's seal.

No, that trauma you faced was not easy,
And God wept that it hurt you so;
But it was allowed to shape your heart
So that into His likeness you'd grow.

You are who you are for a reason,
You've been formed by the Master's rod.
You are who you are, beloved,
Because there is a God!

—Russell Kelfer

Excerpts From Birthfamily Correspondence

Every good deed you do for my daughter should have a reward, and I thank you for your loving care.

* * * * *

I love you all three. (To the child) Please stick to your upbringing. Grow up to be nice, gentle, and kind. I gave you the best parents I could have.

* * * * *

Does she have all her teeth now? She's dear to me. My situation is not suitable for the tremendous task of raising a child. You are very special to me.

* * * * *

I want my child to have a happy home and two loving parents. I did not have a happy home. My parents divorced. I wish I was adopted to a nice Christian couple.

Words can't express how happy and honored I felt to meet you. That was such a wonderful experience for me, and it did help me heal inside. I am so happy and excited for her to be starting such a wonderful life with a loving family. That means so much to me.

* * * * *

Your little boy looks so happy in all the pictures. What kinds of food does he like? How many teeth does he have? Thank you for everything.

* * * * *

The Lord worked in strange ways and I'm sure His will was carried out in this matter. There is no doubt about the depth of love in your home. Your letters have made it easy for me to accept this whole situation.

* * * * *

To a special boy who is loved by many and prayed for. I pray this baby will be a blessing to you in years to come.

* * * * *

A picture drawn by the birthmother to the baby included these verses: Proverbs 22:6 and Ephesians 6:1-3. I love you!

* * * * *

God has truly had a hand in this matter. I've prayed about this and still find peace in my heart about it. I'm entrusting this child into your care. I want you to also know you've found a place in my heart and prayers. This child was not planned for by me but planned for by God, and God wants me to give this gift to you. I'm doing it because I love the two of you and the baby.

* * * * *

Suggested Reading Material

Adopting in America
How to Adopt Within One Year
By Randall Hicks
Wordslinger Press

This book is invaluable. Mr. Hicks is an adoption attorney. He addresses various methods and techniques. There is also a state-by-state review listing laws for that state, adoption attorneys, and agencies. Hundreds of attorneys and agencies listed.

Wordslinger Press
P.O. Box 53
Sun City, CA 92586-9998
Publisher of many adoption books.

Adoptive Parent Association (A.P.A.), same address also publishes a helpful newsletter addressing many adoption issues.

Empty Womb, Aching Hearts
By Marlo Schalesky
Bethany House Publishers

A wonderful book for those still struggling with infertility. It is a very sensitive compilation of stories, helping you realize it is healthy to grieve and how to cope with insensitive remarks others make. It stresses relying on the Lord with your mind, body, and spirit. This is a trial God has allowed to work in us an eternal glory. 2 Corinthians 4:16-18

231

Adopting for Good
By Jorie Kincaid
InterVarsity Press

A practical guide for those considering adoption.

Meditations for Adoptive Parents
By Vernell Klassen Miller
Herald Press

A thirty-day devotional, nicely covering many adoption issues.

The Hand That Rocks the Cradle
Inspirational Meditations for New Mothers
Compiled by Sharilyn Martin and Sue Hooley
Carlisle Press
(available from Christian Light Publications)

Adoption Scrapbook Sheets may be ordered from:
Ronald Rohrer
147 North Shirk Road
New Holland, PA 17557

Inspirational poems and stories relating to adoption and foster parenting on pretty paper, ready to be put into a scrapbook.

A Life in Her Hands
By Shirlee Evans
Herald Press

A poignant story of a birthmother's love, leading her to make an adoption plan.

Cradle of Dreams
By Joseph Bentz
Bethany House Publishers

An excellent story following a young couple through the roller-coaster experience of infertility, treatment, adoption, and biological birth.

When the Womb Is Empty
By Ray and Rebecca Larson
Whitaker House

A complete guide to adoption.

God Gives Me a Family
By Rhoda Bontrager (note author)
Christian Light Publications

A delightful preschool story told by the adopted child.

Adoption for Dummies
By Tracy Barr and Katrina Carlisle
Wiley Publishing Company
Hoboken, NJ 2003

A step-by-step must-read book for anyone wishing to adopt.

Additional Parenting Resources

Christian Family Living
by John Coblentz
Christian Light Publications

Practical, Scriptural instruction in the whole spectrum of godly family living.

Practical Pointers for Training Your Child
by Lloy Kniss
Christian Light Publications

Wisdom from a godly grandfather to aid today's parents in building character.

Adoption Sources

A Loving Choice Adoption Services
1-800-321-2070

   This is operated by a group of three adoptive mothers who network across the U.S.

Adoption Network (domestic and international)
1-574-289-3323

Lavida
Adopting predominately newborn girls from China
150 S. Warner Road, Suite 144
King of Prussia, PA 19406
1-610-688-8008

Orphans Overseas
1-503-297-2006

National Adoption Clearinghouse
   They answer questions and provide information regarding laws, agencies, support groups, etc.
      1-888-251-0075

An Independent Adoption Center
1-800-877-6736

Family to Family Agency
(Domestic and International)
1-909-674-5835

Labor of Love Adoptions
1-888-358-2229

Unique Adoptions
1-909-600-2575

You can always check your yellow pages. Lutheran Social Services, Catholic Charities, and Bethany Christian Services are reputable agencies found in nearly every state.

* * * * * * * * * * * * * * * * * * *

Christian Light Publications, Inc., is a nonprofit, conservative Mennonite publishing company providing Christ-centered, Biblical literature including books, Gospel tracts, Sunday school materials, summer Bible school materials, and a full curriculum for Christian day schools and homeschools. Though produced primarily in English, some books, tracts, and school materials are also available in Spanish.

For more information about the ministry of CLP or its publications, or for spiritual help, please contact us at:

Christian Light Publications, Inc.
P. O. Box 1212
Harrisonburg, VA 22803-1212

Telephone—540-434-0768
Fax—540-433-8896
E-mail—info@clp.org
www.clp.org